NIGERIAN POLITICS

Harper's Comparative Government Series

MICHAEL CURTIS, EDITOR

NIGERIAN POLITICS

JOHN M. OSTHEIMER

NORTHERN ARIZONA UNIVERSITY

1973

HARPER & ROW

Publishers

NEW YORK, EVANSTON, SAN FRANCISCO, LONDON

To Nancy, and

to my mother

CONTENTS

PREFACE

"Nigeria We Hail Thee—
Our own dear native land"
Thus went our National Anthem.
And
With hope our young voices proclaimed . . .
"Though Tribe and Tongue may differ
In brotherhood we stand"
Alas!
Our hopes are gone.

　　　　　　　—Dora Obi Chizea, *"Hail Nigeria,"* 1969

SINCE World War II, the emergence of many new states has greatly affected the study of comparative government and politics. Comparative studies of the structures of government have been altered to make room for analytical studies of change: the political results of "modernization."

In one sense, however, the study of political change has always been part of the comparative approach. Even prior to the introduction of African and Asian studies, students found themselves contrasting the stability of Britain with the turmoils, revolutions, and constitutional innovations of the "newer" states: Germany, France, Italy, and the U.S.S.R. Accustomed to the constancy of political life in his own country, the American student of two decades ago was shocked to discover that political stability is rare. Today's

American student of political science needs no special exposure to the calamities of Weimar or Vichy to recognize that politics, Plato's "master science," does not seem subject to the order of scientific methods.

This book, designed to help students understand some of the reasons for our fluid political world, examines the case of Nigeria. The site of one of the most tragic civil wars of the 1960s, to Americans today "Nigeria" means starving children and mercy missions. But, Nigeria is infinitely more than this. As the giant of tropical Africa, with a population on the scale of France and Britain and extensive natural wealth, Nigeria will undoubtedly have a growing impact on world affairs, alone, or as a likely leader of black Africa in the future.

Ironically, the struggle through a decade of frustration, turmoil, and war has left many Nigerians bewildered. Yet the 1970s promise as many changes as in the years since independence, hopefully with less human suffering.

For the political scientist, this volume of change presents an interesting dilemma, particularly in the creation of a short introductory analysis designed to survey all important aspects of a country's politics. Though I am responsible for the final priorities adopted, several individuals have read parts of the manuscript and have helped me to arrive at different conclusions. I wish to thank in particular Richard Henderson, Peter Kilby, Joseph La Palombara, David Apter, and especially, Derrick Thom, for their insights on what is important for American students to know about Nigerian politics and policies. Finally, I owe a great debt to Mrs. David Langford and to my wife, Nancy, for their patient typing and critical reading.

JOHN M. OSTHEIMER

CHAPTER ONE

Background to Modern Nigeria: Geography and People

NIGERIA HAS BEEN referred to as a "historical accident." Certainly the people of this new state had little to do with the creation of the boundaries that surround them. The final agreement on northern borders was made between Britain and France at the conclusion of an era in which a variety of Nigerian kings and chiefs were cajoled or forced into accepting British authority. After a brief account of the physical setting, this chapter will describe the peoples who found themselves included in the most populous of Britain's African colonies. It will conclude with the main events leading to the formation of "Nigeria" in 1914.

Physical Setting: Location and Ecological Regions

Facing the South Atlantic through the Gulf of Guinea and lacking a strategic position, such as proximity to Suez or command of a much-traveled cape, Nigeria has been far from the mainstreams of world communications. This isolation was reinforced by a wrapper of inhospitable natural barriers: the Sahara and the fever-laden coastal swamps.

Nigeria is a land of climatic and ecological diversity with four distinct physical regions (see Figure 1). Far northern Nigeria contains some sandy, sparsely covered areas of Saharan ecology, but most of the north is savannah (grassy plateau with scanty

Figure 1

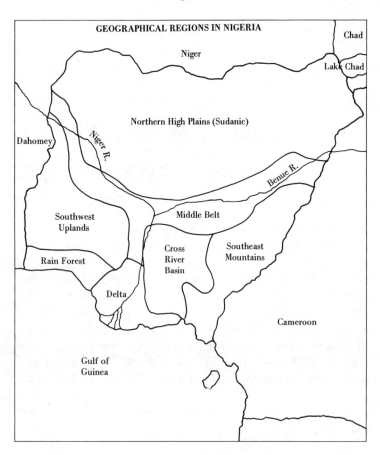

GEOGRAPHICAL REGIONS IN NIGERIA

Chad

Niger

Lake Chad

Northern High Plains (Sudanic)

Dahomey

Niger R.

Benue R.

Southwest
Uplands

Middle Belt

Cross
River
Basin

Southeast
Mountains

Rain Forest

Delta

Cameroon

Gulf of
Guinea

forest) which extends south nearly to the Niger and Benue
Rivers. This northern area is called the "Nigerian Sudan," and
cotton, cattle, and peanuts are its major crops. It is inhabited
by an Islamized agricultural people, the Hausa, who have inter-
mingled with the more traditionally warlike group, the Fulani
(see Figure 3, p. 10).

South of this zone is a transitional ecology known as the
"middle belt," the least developed of Nigeria's major geographic
regions. Its people, dispersed into smaller, distinct ethnic units,

have been kept busy deterring encroachment from the larger groups to the north and south.

The third major ecological region, known as the "Guinea Forest," is an area of high population density and rain-forest agricultural systems, concentrating on yams, bananas, cocoa, and palm products. This rain-forest zone extends nearly to the coast where a swampy mangrove area, varying from 10 to 50 miles wide, intervenes.

Great variations in rainfall and temperature occur among these ecological zones. The Lake Chad area's annual 20 inches of rainfall contrasts sharply to 350 inches in the mountains of the upper Benue. The climate of the forest and coastal areas is not unlike that of Southern Florida. The extreme daily temperature ranges of northern Nigeria are more analogous to conditions in the American Southwest.[1]

On the map, the Niger-Benue River system appears to be a unifying feature. If this had been the case, centers of population and civilization would have reflected this situation. In fact, cataracts, shifting sandbars, seasonal level changes, and the delta's lack of channel definition have restricted communication and trade along this route and delayed contact with the outside world. Other deterrents to movement among the areas occupied by each Nigerian ethnic group are the density of the rain forest and the effects of the tsetse fly, which decimated livestock (especially horses, the main conveyance of the highly organized Hausa-Fulani). It is conceivable that if this tribal system had been able to penetrate the forest area, the diversity of cultural backgrounds and religions in what was to become Nigeria might have been reduced. Some scholars have attempted to stress the natural unity of Nigerian peoples, "drawn from the same 'box of bricks,'" while deemphasizing their traditional isolation.[2] In any case the lack of easy mobility in the forest zone protected the forest cultures from outside dominance. For example, in the stable society of the Ibo people in the eastern rain forest there was

[1] For a recent geographical study, see Reuben K. Udo, *The Geographic Regions of Nigeria*, London: Heinemann, 1970.
[2] See, for example, Okoi Arikpo, *The Development of Modern Nigeria*, Baltimore: Penguin, 1967, p. 13.

little political centralization because they traditionally did not have to fear outside encroachment.

Who Are the Nigerians?

Even authors who have insisted that Nigeria had a firm basis for national unity invariably go on to describe the "great differences between the peoples of the forest and savannah zones." [3] It is true that several Nigerian forest tribes claim descent from one ancestor, the fabled Oduduwa, and that anthropologists have noted other similarities, but it is the variety of traditions that impresses any outside observer. It is essential to understand these diversities in order to comprehend the history of Nigeria's complex governmental structures, and her exciting and frequently chaotic political past.

We would not have to be concerned here about our ability to grasp these essentials if the American setting were not so vitally different from that of most of the "new countries." Based on our own experience, we tend to assume that people within a modern state are held together by an emotional bond, so that a real threat to the security of the country will result in a unity of purpose and in subsequent action. (Our difficulties over Vietnam stem more from doubts about whether communism in Vietnam actually constitutes a real threat than from a weakness in political culture.)

The emotional bond shared by the great majority of Americans derives from our common historical experiences, our mythology of national heroes and villains, and perhaps most of all from the mobility of our people. More important is the enormous area of cultural mutuality, such as our fascination with professional sports, propagated by the mass media. The United States is a "political community," which means that political attitudes are shaped by shared experiences and common personalities that command national attention. Karl Deutsch calls these attitudes "nationalism."

[3] *Ibid.*, ch. 6.

Nationalism is an attitude of mind, a pattern of attention and de-sires. It arises in response to a condition of society and to a particular stage in its development. It is a predisposition to pay far more attention to messages from its members, than to messages from or about any other people. At the same time, it is a desire to have one's own people get any and all values that are available. The extreme nationalist wants his people to have all the power, all the wealth, and all the well-being for which there is any competition. He wants his people to command all the respect and deference from others; he tends to claim all recti-tude and virtue for it, as well as all enlightenment and skill; and he gives it a monopoly of his affection. In short, he totally identifies him-self with his nation. Though he may be willing to sacrifice himself for it, his nationalism is a form of egotism written large.[4]

Deutsch goes on to state that "nationalism," which we can equate to "political integration on a large scale," is by no means a natural human characteristic. Citizens of nations have to be taught "to prefer distant strangers who share our culture and language to any of our next door neighbors who do not." Where feelings of political community have coincided at least roughly with the boundaries of large and populous sovereign systems of government, the potential for concerted activity has existed.

Of course, many of the fruits of such "nation-states" have been negative, for example, the two world wars of this century. But there are significant ways in which political community at the nation-state level has been a positive force. Regardless of the size of their communities, peoples of the true nation-states have succeeded in cooperating to develop the economy, social services, transporta-tion systems, and other features we associate with "progress." The United States and Norway are two outstanding examples.

Cultural and Political Barriers to Unification

In most countries that have emerged since World War II, cultural unity did not serve as the foundation for independent sovereignty, as was frequently the case in European and Anglo-

[4] Karl W. Deutsch, *Politics and Government: How People Decide Their Fate*, Boston: Houghton Mifflin, 1970, p. 80.

American nations. Instead, factors beyond the control of the people of a new country were usually responsible for its shape and identity. The boundaries of most present African states were created in Europe. Therefore, to be a "Nigerian" or "Ghanaian" does not yet suggest a state of mind involving commitment or even possible sacrifice.

Perhaps the greatest irony in this lack of political community is that these same new countries, in order to become modern, are in the greatest hurry to extract sacrifice from their people. Leaders of the new countries have declared war on their own backwardness, and are trying to draw out emotional commitments from populations that have little emotional "support base." Imagine the difference between trying to mobilize Norway for concerted action, and attempting the same procedure with Nigeria. Norway offers few major contrasts, the most significant "minority group" being the Lapps, who account for less than 0.01 percent of the population. Ninety-five percent of Norwegians are Lutheran, and social classes and linguistic differences are not deeply entrenched sources of dissension. The student of Norwegian politics is able to begin with assumptions about Norwegian "national character" or "political style." Since comparative political analysis is in part a search for explanations of why some political systems are more stable than others, the importance of political community must be stressed. Feelings of community breed political consensus, and a high degree of consensus reduces the number and intensity of issues that have the potential to disrupt the system itself. Hence, in the early years of this century, one student of Norwegian politics remarked: "Events that in many countries would be dismissed after a single report in the press remain in Norwegian newspapers for days the subject of public scrutiny and debate." [5] But in the case of a national calamity, trivial issues evaporated as Norwegians gathered for concerted action against Nazi Germany four decades later.

In the language of political communities, Nigeria includes many Norways. None of Nigeria's distinct peoples are clearly

[5] James A. Storing, *Norwegian Democracy*, Boston: Houghton Mifflin, 1963, p. 8.

dominant, as in the case of French dominance over Basque and Breton. Nigeria became independent as a compromise among the three most important ethnic groups, or "tribes," as the Western world is fond of calling them. Before treating these diverse peoples, a semantic problem introduced by the word "tribe" must be confronted.

Europeans and Americans talk of traditional Africa as a land inhabited by "tribes." Therefore, the dissensions in new African countries become in our mind "tribalism." Are they different, however, from the problems of Breton, French Canadian, Ulster, or Scottish "nationalism"? Are not both the African and Western examples cases of separatism by ethnic groups, which form a cultural minority within the country? It seems anachronous to refer to the "nationalism" of three million Welsh in Great Britain, but to the "tribalism" of eight million Ibo within Nigeria. Both are communities that share a sense of identity distinct from that which dominates their country. Yet the point at which they will cease to submit to the majority is hard to discern. Recent events indicate that the Welsh are much more reconciled than the Ibo, but obviously there is no clear dichotomy between nation and tribe.

While the United States and Great Britain are less homogeneous nation-states than the Scandinavian countries, Nigeria cannot be considered a nation-state at all, as it possesses no clearly dominant culture in the important emotional sense.[6] In 1960, Nigeria obtained the formal independence of a state. However, as with most recent new countries, the Nigerian "nation" has still to take shape. Until it does, political stability will be hard to achieve.

This is not to infer that there has been no development of a Nigerian political culture. Research has stressed the sequential nature of political culture development. The molding of attitudes, beliefs, and emotional reactions to life among a community of people is a gradual process of growing specific awareness, honed

---

[6] For an excellent discussion of the semantics of "nation" versus "tribe," see Stanislav Andreski, *The African Predicament: A Study in the Pathology of Modernization*, New York: Atherton, 1968, ch. 4.

by immersion in the community's events. Nigerians were by no means ignorant of their national existence when independence arrived. Data in Chapter Five will explore this subject further, but it is adequate to point out here that probably 90 percent of Nigerians knew the name of their regional Prime Minister, and three-quarters knew who the federal Prime Minister was. Eighty-four percent were able to place Nigeria on a status ladder in comparison with other countries. Nigerians "had, or thought they had, at least some concept of the nationhood of Nigeria."[7] In comparison to Norway, however, attitudes that cause Nigerians to identify with each other as part of a nation seem weaker than subnational affiliations.

Traditional Societies in Nigeria

We are now ready to look closely at the diversities which form the complex bases of Nigerian politics. Until 1967, when the military regime created twelve states, Nigeria was divided into three Administrative Regions, each dominated by one major ethnic group (Figure 2). A fourth region, Midwest, was carved out of the original Western Region in 1962.

The Ibo, who formed the core of Biafra's secessionists, are a traditionally decentralized people, whose political traditions deprecate hierarchy and place an emphasis on participation, discussion, and demonstrated abilities (Figure 3). American advocates of the supremacy of Congress over the Executive would have been at home in central and eastern Iboland. A village assembly of adult males could reject derisively a decision of their lineage leaders. Furthermore, the powers of village government and of larger supravillage entities, circumscribed as they were by popular limits, included few coercive features. Each Ibo individual was educated as to proper social actions; but rather than forcing individual acquiescence, the community placed the burden on each person to maintain Ibo standards. For example, no

[7] Lloyd A. Free, *The Attitudes, Hopes and Fears of Nigerians*, Princeton, N.J.: Institute of International Social Research, 1964, p. 64.

Figure 2

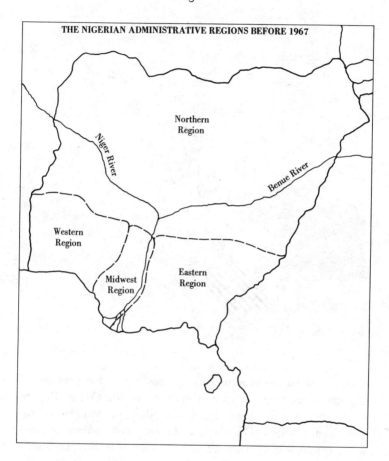

THE NIGERIAN ADMINISTRATIVE REGIONS BEFORE 1967

capital punishment was carried out by the community, but customarily a murderer had a choice between hanging himself or having neighbors harass his extended family.[8]

The contrast between decentralized, participatory politics among some Ibo and the hierarchical systems of the Yoruba and Benin is as vivid as though there were no traditional interchange what-

---

[8] For an account of one variety of Ibo traditional political structure, see M. M. Green, *Ibo Village Affairs*, New York: Praeger, 1964, part I.

Figure 3

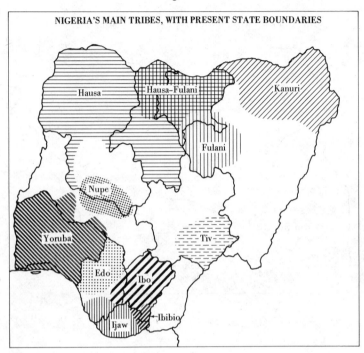

NIGERIA'S MAIN TRIBES, WITH PRESENT STATE BOUNDARIES

soever. Yoruba towns were ranked according to the closeness of the hereditary relationship of their ruler to the Oni of Ife, the king most directly descended from Oduduwa, founder of the traditional capital of Yorubaland. The relative rankings of these kings has long been a source of intra-Yoruba rivalry. The rulers of the more important Yoruba towns (the Alafin of Oyo, the Oni of Ife, the Alake of Abeokuta) possessed highly ritualized authority buttressed by strong armed forces. The high degree of traditional Yoruba urbanization was related to these political developments. Supported by farmland on its periphery, the typical preindustrial Yoruba city required greater organization than did Ibo village life, and the system of interrelated hereditary monarchies provided a degree of legitimacy for that complex organization. Descent from Oduduwa, whom ancient Yoruba had revered as a god, endowed modern Yoruba rulers with great symbolic strength.[9]

The dominant, traditional political system of Northern Nigeria had developed less steadily and with more dramatic alterations, but had reached a degree surpassing even Yoruba. Seven traditional Hausa states dominated the area until 1804, when the pastoral Fulani conquered and assumed control under Uthman dan Fodio. The agricultural Hausa, Islamized to some degree since the fifteenth century, had developed an intricate and hierarchical system based on hereditary kingship. A holy war by the more devout Fulani brought more complete religious unity. A bureaucratic system and centralized political structures were developed under a sultan of Sokoto. Within the sultan's domains, regional "emirs" retained great local power, but the dominant military strength lay in Sokoto, and the subordinate emirs deferred to the sultan. The Hausa-Fulani system after 1810 could be equated to an empire.[10]

Ironically, the more structurally complex traditional systems seemed to provide a poorer preparation for adjustment to British-induced modernization. The example of Ibo and other locally organized southeastern tribes shows that this populist style of government was more adaptable in the long run. This is partially explained by the British view that Ibo decentralization was nothing on which to base modern administration. It is also likely, though, that the Ibo civil servant could learn British methods faster. He had no experience in a large-scale traditional system, and thus no competing model.

Though each of the three natural divisions of Nigeria is dominated by one of the tribal systems described above, many smaller tribes add to the complexity of Nigerian traditional society (Table 1). Northern minorities, like the Nupe on the north banks of the Niger, experienced Fulani invasion as did the Hausa.

[9] On traditional politics in Yorubaland, see Daryll Forde, *The Yoruba-speaking Peoples of Southwestern Nigeria*, London: Oxford University Press, 1950.

[10] An example of traditional government and politics in the Hausa-Fulani emirates is described in M. G. Smith, *Government in Zazzau: 1800–1950*, London: Oxford University Press, 1960.

Table 1. Nigeria's Principal Ethnic Divisions (1963)

Former Region	Major Tribe	1963 Population (in thousands)
North	Hausa	11,653
	Fulani	4,784
	Kanuri	2,259
	Tiv	1,394
East	Ibo	9,246
	Ibibio	2,006
	Ijaw	1,089
West	Yoruba	11,321
Midwest	Edo	955

SOURCE: Adapted from Etienne Van de Walle, "Who's Who and Where in Nigeria," *Africa Report* 15, no. 1 (January 1970): 23.

The Tiv people, however, are one of the less politically hierarchical northern tribes who fought Fulani incursions, remained pagan, and resisted incorporation by the Hausa-Fulani. One-third of those who live in Northern Nigeria are from minority tribes (non-Hausa-Fulani).

Southern Nigerian society is just as diverse. Between the decentralized Ibo and the highly structured Yoruba and Benin existed many culturally distinct groups, with political features adapted from both types to suit local conditions: the small-scale, high centralization of Calabar chiefdoms and the delta city-states. The organization of the delta Ibo, with more political hierarchy, "title" associations, complex descent groups, also demonstrates the difficulty in generalizing about "the Ibo."

It is, therefore, an oversimplification to identify the regions of Nigeria in colonial times with the three dominant ethnic groups. Actually, one of the thorniest modern Nigerian political difficulties, other than competition among the main tribes over control of the federation, has been the preservation of rights for these large regional minorities. Since 1967, civilian and military leaders from the smaller tribes have taken control of the federal system, and the prospect of further anxiety over this issue has lessened.

Language

Considering the importance of a national language as a bond of unity in a nation, Nigeria can be more easily understood. Nigeria is more linguistically complex than most of us can imagine. Within Europe, the main languages, French, German, Spanish, and English, are all intonational Indo-European languages. In Nigeria, Yoruba and Ibo are tonal Niger-Congo languages, Hausa, although it has some tones, is an intonational Afro-Asiatic tongue. These differences are significant, assuming either attempts by Ibo and Yoruba to learn Hausa, or the reverse situation. As a *lingua franca* for governmental affairs, English has provided one way around this barrier to communication. But in a country with 10 percent literacy in any language, political participation is quite likely to suffer from misinformation and misunderstanding.

Another complicating factor is that the British use of English was not equal throughout the colony. Though some southerners were employed in the northern civil service, a greater proportion of administrators in the North were indigenous civil servants, who were allowed to use Hausa among their subjects. Colonial administrators in the southern regions were more frequently English, or Africans from other regions who could not speak the local language and had to use English.

The cultural, social, and familial differences between the predominantly Moslem north, and the south with its large number of Christians and pagans, are enormous. There is an additional difference in the role of women. In Hausa culture, women were considered chattel, secluded from public sight according to the Moslem practice of "purdah."[11] Even as late as Nigeria's First Republic, 1963–1966, women in northern Nigeria were denied the franchise. Women among the southern Nigerians might be more likely to favor the "women's lib" movement, but would

[11] On the status of women in traditional northern Nigeria, see Mary Smith, *Baba of Karo: A Woman of the Moslem Hausa*, New York: Praeger, 1964.

surely have less reason. They have exercised a continuing influence, spurred on by a modern commercial outlook, vibrant political organizations, and a willingness to participate by voting and joining groups.

Awareness of Nigeria's ethnic diversity is fundamental to an understanding of the problems there during the past decade. Incomplete political community is a barrier to unity in many new states, but perhaps Nigeria's situation is unique. Ethnic divisions are so deep that recent developments, not inevitable elsewhere, have been exploited by these differences.[12]

Argument among some political scientists centers on the role of tribalism as a force causing events in new African nations. To some, tribalism is the root of every problem. Perhaps a more balanced view is that today's educated leaders of political parties recognize tribalism's potential as a vehicle for mass support. "In Africa, violent passions flow easily into tribalistic channels." [13]

The Formation of Nigeria

It has traditionally been assumed that a high proportion of the tribulations experienced by Africa's new states are the result of the arbitrary boundaries drawn by Europeans and since legitimized by the passage of time. Two reasons are usually advanced for this argument: that the boundaries split up some African tribes, laying the groundwork for future tension between current countries; and that various (sometimes hostile) tribes were lumped together, creating the basis for dissension within each new country. The first of these topics will be dealt with in a later chapter on Nigeria's relations with her neighbors. The second is the major historical fact pertinent to this chapter: Nigeria was an arbitrary creation.

[12] P. C. Lloyd, "The Ethnic Background to the Nigerian Crisis", in S. K. Panter-Brick, ed., *Nigerian Politics and Military Rule: Prelude to the Civil War*, London: Athlone Press, 1970, p. 1.

[13] For an amplification of this thesis, see Richard L. Sklar, "Political Science and National Integration—A Radical Approach," *The Journal of Modern African Studies* 5, no. 1 (1967).

The British were not the first Europeans to be interested in the Niger delta. Before explorers had established the connection between the coastal "oil rivers" and the Niger (known to exist far inland but believed to flow west), several European countries had vied for control of the delta as a source of trade.

For over two centuries, trade had been dominated by the export of slaves. In 1807, when the slave trade was declared illegal by the British Parliament, interest turned toward replacing slave traffic with "legitimate trade." British traders, ensconced in riverside posts in the delta and in coastal forts adjacent to the tribal centers of trade, demanded protection from the British Crown. They needed to control inland areas so they could cut costs inflated by African and Arab middlemen. During the middle of the nineteenth century, Niger discoveries and increased demand for palm oil brought the area to the forefront of British public interest. A system of consular protection for British traders was set up on the island of Fernando Po. By 1853, the consul's power was increased to include Lagos on the mainland (Figure 4). During the 1850s, consuls worked with British traders to eliminate African competition. The strategic value of Lagos, a natural harbor within easy reach of the entire delta area, then became obvious. Lagos provided a base from which to crush Dahomey, the single remaining West African slave kingdom. Stabilizing Yoruba politics would hinder Dahomey's ability to capitalize on civil war among the Yoruba cities by extracting many Yorubas for sale to the slavers.

The British consul forced a Treaty of Cession from the King of Lagos in 1861. With Lagos under control, adjacent areas were declared "protectorates" and the British consuls widened their sphere of influence. Most of the Yoruba cities objected vigorously to this encroachment, and their resistance limited until the 1880s the access to Yorubaland set up by the Lagos consul-trader alliance.

British government policy during that period was not always wholeheartedly imperialistic, an important point to keep in mind in understanding the development of the former British colonies. The hesitant, piecemeal construction of her empire

Figure 4

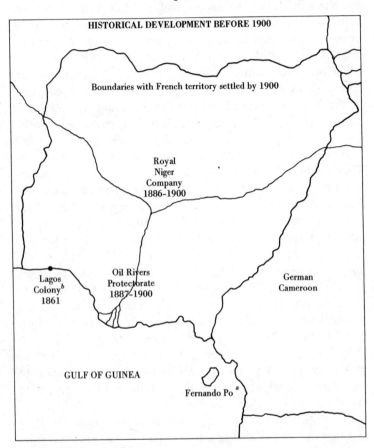

HISTORICAL DEVELOPMENT BEFORE 1900

Boundaries with French territory settled by 1900

Royal
Niger
Company
1886–1900

Lagos
Colony[b]
1861

Oil Rivers
Protectorate
1887–1900

German
Cameroon

GULF OF GUINEA

Fernando Po [a]

[a]Fernando Po is now part of the independent country of Equatorial Guinea. A Portuguese possession until 1778, the island was ceded to Spain, who ruled until 1968 with one break in her dominion: From 1827 until 1844, Britain was allowed to use the island as a naval base against the slave trade. Even after negotiations to sell the island to Britain collapsed, Spain appointed an Englishman as governor. Spain began to reassert actual control after 1858.

[b]Lagos was assigned to the consul stationed in Fernando Po in 1853. It was formally annexed in 1861.

derived from the complex international role of Victorian Britain. Masters of the seas and of their trade, both Liberal and Tory governments disliked the prospect of expensive administration over areas from which profits were already being extracted quite successfully in the competition with other European nations. The government of France, by 1830, or Germany after 1870, had more reason to value the creation of trade monopolies through governmental control. They realized their merchants would be at a great disadvantage competing with the entrenched British. Cecil Rhodes in southern Africa, and Sir George Goldie on the Niger, are examples of British merchant administrators who had to convince politicians that British commercial interests could not successfully compete under free trade conditions with the government-supported companies of the French or Germans.

This is a noteworthy historical point, because the tardiness of Britain's "colonial awakening" in West Africa resulted in the isolation of her colonies from each other. Nonetheless, Britain's maritime strength in the early nineteenth century assured her of choice possessions—the Niger and Volta River Valleys peopled by some of the most vigorous of West African tribes, and endowed with resources and wealth.

Britain's hesitation in West Africa also stemmed from her zeal in protecting the "more important" areas. The 1882 revolt in Egypt brought a vigorous military response because supply lines to strategic parts of the Empire in India and Asia were threatened. From the time the Suez Canal was opened in 1869 until the 1880s, West African problems never evoked the same strong British stance, for that area was not perceived to be as crucial to British interests. Therefore, though France and Germany both envied Britain's rich possession on the Gulf of Guinea, to Britain, Nigeria was of secondary importance.[14]

[14] Britain's comparative lethargy in overall African colonization should not obscure the fact that, on the scene, vigorous efforts were made by Royal Niger Company officials, such as Goldie and Frederick Lugard, to protect the Niger area from French intrusion. These exciting events are recounted in Michael Crowder, *A Short History of Nigeria*, New York: Praeger, 1966, ch. 12.

At a conference in Berlin in 1884–1885, the British government had agreed to consign most of Equatorial and West Africa to France, Germany, and King Leopold of the Belgians. Those powers had in return recognized British hegemony over four West African areas: three river valleys (Gambia, Volta, Niger) and Freetown, whose port was used for a century as a depository for freed slaves. In 1886, Britain chartered the Royal Niger Company (RNC), a virtual government in every sense of the word save for foreign affairs. RNC's dual purpose was to exploit the resources of the Niger area and to govern to the degree necessary for commercial activity. But the company's expansion toward the north and west aroused hostile reactions from French interests operating in those frontiers. While RNC could not maintain effective control beyond a rough circle some 200 miles around the Niger-Benue confluence, the Company claimed spheres of influence well north, west, and east of that area. The Oil Rivers Protectorate over the delta south of RNC control was established in 1887 (Figure 4). Dissatisfaction with the RNC's administration (where it was established) and with the Company's failure to extend control to surrounding areas led to the end of RNC charter in 1900. In the same year formal boundary agreements were concluded with France.

To conclude, before 1900, control over Britain's Niger possessions was exercised by three different agencies: RNC controlled inland river valleys and claimed to rule the vast surrounding areas; the Foreign Office ruled the delta protectorate; and the Colonial Office was responsible for Lagos Colony. In 1900, the Colonial Office took control of all Britain's Niger possessions, but not until 1906 were the Oil Rivers Protectorate (since 1900 called "Southern Nigeria") and the Lagos Colony combined. Finally, in 1914, territory north of the Niger and Benue Rivers was added to those southern holdings to form the "Colony and Protectorate of Nigeria." Obviously, only the misinformed would speak of concerted planning by a British government committed to the development of "Nigeria" before 1914. Disparate Nigerian peoples were finally about to experience living within a single administrative system for the first time just as the tradition-forged nationalistic interests of Europe were squaring off for World War I.

It should be apparent that, compared to modern nation-states such as England, France, or Germany (who have had their own difficulties), Nigeria did not have an auspicious debut. No "Bismarck" appeared to unify the diverse Nigerian tribes. No seventeenth-century "settlements," equivalent to those made between York and Lancaster or between Catholic and Protestant, were made between Nigerian regions and the various tribes. No Louis XIV ever "encouraged" Nigeria's dozens of ethnic units to acknowledge one central authority, nor did common linguistic and cultural traditions exist to support such political events, had they occurred. A Nigerian "nation" had still to be created. It was indeed doubtful that any foreign power could preside over the processes just outlined. But by 1914, had not World War I intervened, Britain was ready to try.

CHAPTER TWO

Background to Modern Nigeria:
Constitutional Development

By 1914 BRITISH INTERESTS on the Niger had been amalgamated as the "Colony and Protectorate of Nigeria." Under Governor-General Sir Frederick Lugard, the process of integrating the administration of the disparate areas was slowly begun. Unfortunately, the attempt suffered several reversals after 1945, and important issues that would eventually divide Nigerians were never squarely faced before independence. In this chapter, the effects of the colonial era on Nigeria are surveyed through analyses of the constitutional developments, the theories and operation of colonial rule, and the impact of colonialism on traditional politics. The chapter ends with a survey of the relevant social and political changes wrought by British rule.

Constitutional Developments Preceding Independence

Nigeria began as a collection of contiguous British possessions, and became independent as a loose federation on the Australian model. After World War I, British administrators tried to unify Nigeria's three principal areas into the Administrative Regions shown on Figure 2, and some progress was indeed made. Lugard's proposal of amalgamation, largely followed by the government established in 1914, gave the Governor-General final authority, limited only by his responsibility to the Colonial Office in London. To aid Lugard in Lagos, the Executive Council was enlarged and an advisory assembly, called the Nigerian Council, was formed. Consisting of 42 seats, 12 reserved for Nigerians, this Council had little influence and is recounted as a failure, meeting only 7 times in as many years! More will be said in Chapter Six about the development of legislative and advisory councils during Nigeria's colonial period. This chapter will concentrate on divisions of power between Lagos and the Regions, and on other aspects of Nigeria's administrative federalism. An obvious result of the federal colonial structure was a failure to prepare Nigeria for independence because the survival of ethnic groups was encouraged, a development that hindered the growth of a feeling of being "Nigerians" with common problems.

Detailed reasons for the British proclivity toward the federal solution, ill-suited to virtually all non-Western societies—India, Malaysia, the Caribbean, South Arabia, Central Africa—belong to another story. Briefly, the Nigerian case can be seen as part of a vicious circle that widened during the decades of British rule. British involvement elsewhere in the world, and the consequent secondary importance of Nigeria in the eyes of British officials led to a theory of low-cost government eventually glorified by the term "indirect rule." In order to keep costs down and maintain peace easily, local rulers, fresh from defeat and humiliation at the hands of a British force, were reinstated as the colonial government's agents. It is not our purpose to moralize, from the advantage of hindsight, about "wrong" British policies. Britain was preoccupied with more important world matters, and as statements by Lugard and others reveal, the British really believed (correctly from their short-term point of view) that rule based on existing structures was likely to be more peaceful and successful.

Lugard's technique of ruling after 1914 was to delegate authority to a lieutenant-governor for Northern Nigeria at Kaduna, and one for Southern Nigeria at Lagos. The two autonomous provinces produced separate budgets and mobilized their own police, health services, prisons, schools, and other basic functions.

Wherever possible, lieutenant-governors were encouraged to utilize indigenous rulers. Some powers were centralized under the Governor-General, including railways and coal mines, the military, treasury, telecommunications, and judiciary, but Lugard tried to federalize the administration of most activities. To balance this apparent recognition of the diversity within Nigeria, however, we should recall that the two provinces were themselves arbitrary creations, and that the amalgamation was effected primarily as a measure to reduce the overall costs of the new railway connecting the North with the coastal areas.

Clifford Constitution, 1922

The Clifford Constitution of 1922, named for the governor who replaced Lugard in 1918, is usually remembered for the creation of the Legislative Council (LEGCO) and inclusion in it of the first elected African members in British Africa. Much more significant for later Nigerian development was the exclusion of Northern Nigeria from this new LEGCO. The southern-dominated population of Lagos began immediately to compete in the organization of political machinery to win the three elective positions that were to represent that city. The northerners, who were not given such an opportunity, however, continued to assume that budgetary allotments would be decreed for them and were not a subject of political contention. Exposure to these issues would have raised the level of political sophistication among the northern elite, but colonial decisions were conspiring to retard development even further. Christian mission schools, crucial to southern Nigerian modernization, were excluded from northern Moslem areas, and education lagged accordingly.

Richards Constitution, 1946

The effects of the absence of northern representatives from the Clifford Constitution LEGCO were considerable. Involvement in national level lawmaking would have stimulated northern political awareness and organization, and might have prevented some of the later fears on the part of northern leaders of the threat posed by the more politically advanced South. Equally important, a northern political presence might well have diverted a greater share of budget allocation to the North, thereby narrowing the gap between the educational and social levels of North and South, while introducing political techniques. This situation was remedied in the Richards Constitution of 1946, but by then North and South had already been set on differing courses. Though Governor Sir Arthur Richards's tactics of introducing the document as a *fait accompli* were politically destructive, he recognized the necessity of changing a system "unsuited for expansion on a Nigerian basis." [1]

Growing southern Nigerian nationalism made British governors aware that the North would have difficulty competing successfully in post-World War II Nigeria. Increasing political roles for Nigerians, leading eventually to internal self-government, indicated northern ignorance would be costly. The 1946 Constitution set up Regional Assemblies to channel demands to a federal LEGCO in Lagos. One reason for this decision was that the poor command of the English language by most northerners would work to their disadvantage, if the single federal LEGCO were merely enlarged to include the North.

Since these Regional Councils for Eastern, Western, and Northern Nigeria had only advisory functions, it would not be true to say that Nigeria had become a federation by virtue of the 1946 Constitution. The governor retained the balance of power at the center, though the countryside was administered according to the level of development of each of Nigeria's Regions. In essence, the Richards Constitution instituted a system of advisory councils that would make policy recommendations at more local levels.

[1] Kalu Ezera, *Constitutional Developments in Nigeria*, Cambridge: Cambridge University Press, 1960, p. 66. See also Babatunde A. Williams, "Constitutions and National Unity in Nigeria: A Historical and Analytical Study," *Journal of Business and Social Studies* 1, no. 1 (September, 1968): 51–74.

Administratively, the division of Nigeria into three Regions dates back to 1939. The Richards Constitution reaffirmed this division in 1946. Central direction from Lagos remained strong, but the retention of Regional divisions did strengthen the ground-work for the sectional nature of Nigerian nationalism. As Chapter Four will show, Nigerian political awareness rose rapidly during the 1940s. A greater role for the central "advisory assembly" might have curtailed the localism that began to divide Nigerian anticolonialist politicians. Undeniably, this would have been hard on the less sophisticated northerners for a time, but it is reason-able to assume that, realizing the high stakes at issue in any central legislative structure, northerners probably would have quickly acquired the requisite political skills from that time onward.

MacPherson Constitution, 1951

Vigorous Nigerian anticolonialism forced a shortening of the projected operating period for the Richards Constitution. The colonial government had intended to make any revisions that proved necessary after nine years. However, three years of strong criticism, coupled with the resignation of Governor Richards, brought plans for a new constitutional formula. The new colonial administrator, Governor Sir John MacPherson, proved more open to Nigerian opinion. His government found that Nigerians generally favored more devolution of policy making into Regional hands. Consequently, the 1951 constitution transformed the re-gions, which had been merely administrative divisions, into com-plete political and governmental systems with executive councils and legislative assemblies. In addition, direct election to the central legislature was ended: The regional legislatures would provide the federal delegates.

Ending direct popular election to the central legislature em-phasized the regional context of Nigeria's political awakening. At the same time, this regional focus deepened because of the decentralization of the new constitutional provisions. The most significant political result of the 1951 MacPherson Constitution was the attention each of the new political parties subsequently gave to its own region. Control over most of the important functional tasks of government (for example, agriculture, education, local industries, social welfare, health, local courts) was specifically given over to regional governments. Still, significant powers were retained by the central government. The Constitution reserved for the Federal Legislature the right to object to regional laws, and the Governors could veto bills that were, in his view, outside of regional jurisdiction.

Soon after the 1951 Constitution went into effect, the assumption that it was only temporary, coupled with a series of crises, made the system unworkable. In early 1953, Eastern Region legislators brought their government's operation to a standstill by defeating the appropriations bill. Though the ministers had clearly lost the confidence of the majority in the Eastern Region Legislature, they defied parliamentary procedure and refused to resign. Because the MacPherson Constitution had no provision for dissolving a regional legislature, the crisis was prolonged. Finally, after the Constitution was amended in May 1953, the Eastern House of Assembly was dissolved, a new legislature elected, and a new government formed from the parliamentary majority.

While the Eastern Region was in turmoil, a political crisis within the central government rocked the entire colony. In a rare display of cohesion, Yoruba and Ibo legislators backed a demand for "self-government by 1956." Northern Parliamentarians, however, were not enthusiastic about competing so soon with the more politically advanced southerners unless the British shield remained. Many of the northern legislators, highly educated and perceptive people, realized that mass political organization would become extremely significant in the new Nigeria and that their own political machinery was relatively traditional when compared to the impressive political mobilization of the Yoruba Action Group or the Ibo dominated National Council of Nigeria and the Cameroons. Since the northern delegates could have defeated the "self-government by 1956" motion as they controlled half the seats, the southerners chose to verbally abuse the members of the cabinet, and then walk out of the federal legislature. When northern members of Parliament emerged from the hall, they required police protection against the angry Lagos crowds.

Northern leaders were understandably alienated by this turn of events, and riots in the North followed as the enraged Hausas retaliated against the southerners living outside their walled cities. The Northern Region government then proposed an "Eight-Point Programme" that was distinctly confederal in nature. Only minimal central government powers would remain, such as co-ordination of transportation and postal service. Lagos would become neutral territory.

The resignation of the four central government ministers from the Western Region meant that the central government could no longer continue constitutionally, since all three regions were supposed to have representation in it. With public confidence in the system growing visibly weaker, the Colonial Office in London indicated that discussions should begin on a new constitution.[2]

Lyttleton Constitution, 1954

At conferences in London and Lagos during 1953 and 1954, the nature of government in Nigeria was substantially turned away from central power toward confederated power. Powers in the hands of the central government were made specific, as were the list of "concurrent powers" held mutually by the regions and the center, with important residual powers being reserved for the regions. Other provisions tipped the scale in favor of the regions. Rather than continue to divide revenues in a manner that would reflect each region's developmental needs, the principle of "derivation" was introduced, which meant that a region's budgetary allocations were roughly the same as the amount it

[2] On the interplay between constitutional change and nationalist development between 1918 and 1954, see James S. Coleman, *Nigeria: Background to Nationalism*, Berkeley: University of California Press, 1960.

had the capacity to collect in revenues. To complete the significant developments of 1954, the civil service and judicial systems were decentralized and placed in the hands of the regional governments.

It is important to understand how the various participants contributed to these constitutional discussions. In 1946, when nationalist organization was in its early stages, British statesmen played a central role in every stage of decision making; the Richards Constitution was a surprise even to informed Nigerians. Nigerians were much more significant in the drafting of the 1951 MacPherson Constitution, and were dominant in drawing up the Lyttleton Constitution of 1954. Their "nationalisms" were obviously regionalist versions of anticolonialism, with the British role in 1953–1954 that of referee. Lyttleton gave in to the decentralization of powers and structures, and only intervened when openly secessionist statements were made by one of the parties.

The development of Nigerian political ideas and organization will be explained later. It is crucial to note at this point that as the constitutional development of Nigeria came under the influence of Nigerian politicians and came to reflect their views, divisive trends began to dominate, and British administration provided the major unifying influence. The Lyttleton Constitution of 1954, the first truly federal system since "Nigeria" came into existence in 1914, was, as *West African Pilot* wrote, "the handiwork of Nigerians." [3] In some of its major features, the Lyttleton Constitution was rather like the United States Constitution's Tenth Amendment. Powers not specifically bestowed on the federal government are the province of the states. However, the list of concurrent powers was impressive, and many observers hoped the Nigerian Federal Government would achieve the growth in central power that has occurred in the United States, particularly in view of the stated desires of Nigerian politicians for rapid economic development. These trends were anticipated from another point of view as well. Strong central initiative would have aided the growth of a sense of "Nigerian"

[3] Ezera, *Constitutional Developments*, p. 66.

identity and common purpose. Indeed, the provision that the federal law would prevail if the regional and federal laws came into conflict in a concurrent area should have furthered the growth of federal government influence. British administrators and Nigerian politicians seem to have interpreted this constitutional balance in different ways, however. Lyttleton hoped it would redress the balance toward the center, while most Nigerian leaders sensed that if they controlled a regional legislature and were able to somehow incapacitate the central legislature, the central government would not be able to threaten the regions with use of concurrent powers. They tacitly but correctly assumed that this would occur with the withdrawal of Nigerian civil servants and politicians to each respective region.

As one Nigerian scholar has noted, "the 1954 constitution was the kernel of all further constitutional changes, which culminated in the establishment of the Federal Republic of Nigeria on 1 October 1963." [4] Responding to this change, the Federal government after 1954 was composed increasingly of the lieutenants of the party bosses, who chose to remain in their regional capital. The same was true of the civil service. British expatriate administrators were called on increasingly to staff the Federal civil service, replacing Nigerians who were recalled to assume leading roles in the civil service of their own region. It was more than likely under these circumstances that initiative would come from the regions rather than the center.

To complete this review of constitutional developments up to independence, internal self-government was bestowed on the two southern regional governments in 1957. Nigerian politicians serving as regional premiers and their Executive Councils (cabinets) could generally make law without veto by the British Regional Governor (who had become a figurehead). These events furthered the trend toward regional orientation in Nigerian politics, with Yoruba, Ibo, and Hausa-Fulani dominating the three regional governments. Quite naturally, with this crucial political issue resolved to the advantage of the three dominant ethnic groups,

---

[4] Arikpo, *Development of Modern Nigeria*, p. 82.

attention finally focused on ways to protect the substantial minorities within each region who were becoming increasingly aware of their precarious position.

To summarize, particularly after World War II, when Britain and other imperial powers gradually began to view their role in the colonies more seriously, tasks of educational, social, and economic development dictated more concerted, centralized administrative effort. However, particularly in African colonies, political activity stimulated by postwar changes frequently took a regional or tribal form. Antiimperialism became the vehicle for superficial unity among politicians in the colonies, but the inherent lack of deep, nationalistic feelings kept politicians divided.

In some cases, the potential antagonists were not of equal strength; the Ashanti in Ghana were not able to overcome the nationalist initiative from non-Ashanti educated elite, and centralized government succeeded. In Nigeria, tribes considered each other as mutually powerful threats. Britain, with no written constitution of its own at all, hoped that constitutional provisions would hold Nigeria together long enough for a sense of mutual identity and experience to provide a more permanent bond. Ironically, federal constitutions, perhaps more than unitary ones, depend on the will of people to cooperate with each other. In unitary states, minorities concentrated in one area might be controlled forcefully through the central government's monopoly of power. Truly federal states rely more on voluntary cooperation.

Nigeria in the Context of Comparative Federalism

To understand a federation's prospects for success, it is necessary to examine the way powers are divided among the levels of government. Students of modern federalism have been inclined to locate the "residual powers" and assess their importance. If the balance of powers appears clearly on the side of the central government, that constitution would be classified as "quasifederal" (bordering on "unitary") but if the regional governments control the most important powers, the term "confederal" is used. The constitutional structure itself is by no means enough to explain the prospects for successful federation; the role of political parties and the attitudes of the people are even more significant factors. The contribution that can be made by structures as decreed by the constitution is indicated by William Riker:

> If a federalism is centralized, then the ruler(s) of the federation have and are understood to have greater influence over what happens in the society as a whole than do all the rulers of the subordinate governments. And, having this influence, they tend to acquire more. Thus, an identifying feature of centralized federalism is the tendency, as time passes, for the rulers of the federation to overawe the rulers of the constituent governments. Conversely, if a federalism is initially peripheralized, the rulers of the subordinate governments tend to acquire more; and thus an identifying feature of peripheralized federalism is the tendency, eventually, for the rulers of constituent governments to overawe the ruler(s) of the federation.[5]

It was Riker's view that "Peripheralized federalisms . . . can hardly be expected to provide effective government." Examining Nigeria in 1963, he concluded: "it is surprising that the federation exists at all." [6]

Development of Nigeria's Political Environment

Nigeria's constitutional landmarks are not by themselves a sufficient background for our analysis of present politics and government. We must also examine social, economic, and political changes that accompanied and sometimes fostered the trends toward decentralization, which accelerated during the last decade of colonial rule. Generally, the tighter economic links between European countries and African colonies after World War II resulted in social and demographic changes which had an impact

---

[5] William H. Riker, Federalism: Origin, Operation, Significance, Boston: Little, Brown, 1964, p. 7. A political geographer classified Nigeria's First Republic as a "compromise federation." See Harm deBlij, A Systematic Political Geography, New York: Wiley, 1967.

[6] Ibid., p. 31.

on internal political awakening. In Nigeria, the "colonial period" in a unified sense was unusually short, even compared with other African cases, and the economic and social transitions were abrupt. Nigerian political activity reflected these conditions.

The 47-year period from 1914–1960 was not a long life for a colony. Britain's brief tutelage over the "Colony and Protectorate of Nigeria" contrasts with her 80-year rule over India, and her century of reign over the Gold Coast (Ghana). To add further perspective, these decades were by no means solidly devoted to the matter of Nigerian development. Such events as World Wars I and II and the intervening depression, left only about two decades, in installments at that, for the policies of advancement! Under these circumstances, it is not surprising that Nigeria lagged behind many other British and French colonies.

One long period of possible development, 1918–1929, was handicapped by colonial experimentation. According to Lugard's theory of the "dual mandate," Britain had two basic tasks: to advance the "native races" in her colonies and to open the resources of each colony for use by the industrial countries. There is some irony in Lugard's choice of procedures, however. Historians of colonial administration have labeled the British approach "indirect rule"; the prototype of this form of colonial government was found in northern Nigeria. Indirect rule was quite logical in one sense: If the traditional political system could serve as intermediary between the people and the new reality of British domination, prospects for peaceful operation would be enhanced. However, the Africans were likely to accept the legitimacy of their own rulers only if those emirs, sultans, chiefs, or kings actually appeared to have a participating role in the formation of policy. British policy thus had to move cautiously in order not to make its indigenous underlings appear to be puppets. The goals of the dual mandate were difficult to achieve under these circumstances.

Faced after 1914 with the task of amalgamating two different colonial systems, Lugard opted to try the northern system in the southern parts of Nigeria. The alternative would have been to do away with the traditional northern emirates and their bureaucracy, but the expense of their replacement by direct British administration would have been prohibitive. Therefore, the Northern Nigerian native administration and provincial constitutional systems were transplanted to replace British-model structures that had been operating in Southern Nigeria. Amalgamation proved difficult and not very successful under these terms. By 1933 all duplicated departments had been integrated, but, especially in Eastern Nigeria, where the traditional function of the chief was circumscribed by popular participation and consent, native administration based on the northern model was a dismal failure. Direct administration was necessarily reintroduced in many southern areas, with an emphasis on training Nigerians for roles within the modern administrative structure.

Financially, the pace of Nigeria's progress was determined by the dictum that colonies should not be a burden on England. For four decades after the creation of Nigeria in 1914, no net investments were made by Britain. All road, railway, educational, and administrative developments had to be financed from local taxation. Ironically, British power was most directly applied in eastern Nigeria, which was soon providing the weakest public services because of its poor tax base. In the northern cities, where a strong traditional emirate system had no trouble taxing the people, Nigeria's best hospitals, roads, and other public developments were built. Except for a few railways and ports managed from the center, progress depended on the tremendous variations in the efficiency of local administration. Again, a sense of irony is necessary to understand the Nigerian system: As in all colonies, the governor and his administration were unquestionably in command of budgetary and other important policies. It is true that the Nigerian Council (after 1922, the Legislative Council, LEGCO) was empowered to take part in the legislative process. However, this structure was only important in Southern Nigeria, for in the North the governor made policy directly. Thus, southern Nigerians were thrust into the governmental process at higher levels of decision making earlier than in the North—a crucial factor in the South's more rapid political advancement. However, as indicated above, the northern administration was responsible during the intervening period for progress in some fields of social services and transportation.

The Colonial Development and Welfare Act of 1940 marked the end of locally balanced budgets in British colonies. Though expenditure commitments were small under the 1940 act, Britain had at least abandoned the idea that colonies must pay for themselves. After World War II, when Britain was first able to carry out her intentions for colonial expenditures, plans were drawn up on the basis of only $15 million a year for the decade 1946–1955. The last 15 years of colonial rule did witness more extensive investment in roads, agriculture, and schools. Luckily the quickening pace of Nigerian economic development was not dependent on these small expenditures. Insatiable demand for Nigeria's primary products served as the greatest stimulus.

At first, the postwar development surge promised changes on a planned basis throughout the colony. Income from taxes, excises, and exports from richer areas was used to promote development wherever the needs were most obvious. Then, as Nigeria awakened politically, each Region demanded more control over the uses of its resources and income, and planning on the basis of developmental needs gave way to the principle of "derivation"—that money be allotted to each Region according to its ability to produce revenues. This hindered development in the poorer East and left more resources for the richer West and North. By 1954 the principle of "derivation" was receiving far greater emphasis than were the requisites of "need." One of the greatest difficulties of this policy was that the growing demand by Ibos for education produced a legion of clerks, teachers, and semiskilled gradu- ates who were unemployed within their own, poorer region. Spurred by land scarcity in Iboland, Ibo emigration toward the North, West, and Lagos grew.

The impact of comparatively rapid postwar development, especially the demand for cocoa, tin, vegetable oils, and columbite, and the general expansion of the trade sector, was considerable. During the period 1945–1960, the value of Nigeria's exports increased nearly 10 times, and this growth was not as fragile as in colonies dependent on a single crop. However, since Nigeria was not in a position to monopolize the supply of any of its exports, market fluctuations have helped to determine the value of her export earnings. After the Korean War, for example, demand for Nigerian metals dropped drastically.

The Marketing Board system was able to reduce earning fluctuations for some of the colony's products. Marketing Boards were government-administered cooperatives that purchased crops from individual member farmers, and managed the sale of the entire export-directed production. To moderate the effects that fluctuations in world commodity prices would have on the individual farmer, they built up balances to pay him an "average price" for his crops. The Marketing Boards also served to dispense information about agricultural techniques and to collect taxes.

Response of Africans to Colonial Development

There were wide differences in the reactions of Nigerians to the new economic challenges after 1924, and to the accompanying social upheavals. A very small number of Nigerians resisted the changes. Many more quickly saw the possible advantages for themselves, their families, and their villages. In the South, economic activity was already firmly based on trade with Europe. Palm oil had replaced slaves as the chief export in the nineteenth century and during the short colonial era other plantation crops, small industries, and handicrafts were easily introduced into the area.

Ibo reactions to British rule took several forms. British indirect rule was generally ineffective because the Ibo, "jealous of their legislative authority," resisted the dictates of British-appointed chiefs.[7] Evidence of the administrative failure in Eastern Nigeria was the Aba riots of 1929: Dozens of dissenting Ibo women, who guessed that assessment of their property meant taxation, were shot. In 1931, the system in Eastern Nigeria was partially revised to allow for more participation at the village level. The

[7] Victor C. Uchendu, The Igbo of Southeast Nigeria, New York: Holt, Rinehart and Winston, 1965, p. 42.

Ibo adjusted speedily to the new setting based on village councils. One ethnographer of the Ibo explained their adaptiveness as a consequence of the varying ecological settings, population pressure, and lack of centralized political structure, and added:

The Ibo for a long time have willingly incorporated small numbers of other peoples with different cultures into their social groupings. Strangers are readily adopted and provided with land; new religious shrines are acquired by trade and purchase; new forms of title societies and religious ceremonies are readily incorporated. The Ibo had been accepting new cultural forms and new personnel for many years prior to European contact.[8]

Compared to the Ibo, other Nigerian ethnic groups adapted less speedily and completely to the colonial situation. Cash crops took hold slower in the North especially, serving less as an uprooter of traditional organization there than in the southern areas, where cocoa and palm oil products introduced many Africans to the money economy. There were other features of colonial rule that served to change facets of northern society, but on the whole, the impact of colonialism was mollified by the protection of traditional religion and social hierarchy provided by indirect rule. The result was what one observer has labeled a "stable symbiosis of modern and traditional elements." Northern Nigeria neither rejected completely colonialism's changes, nor totally accepted modernization's features.[9]

The impact of economic changes wrought by colonialism was blunted in Western Nigeria by the traditional nature of Yoruba urbanization. The disquieting effects of modern urbanization, which created many uprooted Ibos, were absorbed with less difficulty by the Yoruba.

[8] Simon Ottenberg, "Ibo Receptivity to Change," in William R. Bascom and Melville J. Herskovits, eds., *Continuity and Change in African Cultures*, Chicago: University of Chicago Press, 1962, p. 140.

[9] C. S. Whitaker, Jr., *The Politics of Tradition, Continuity and Change in Northern Nigeria, 1946–1966*, Princeton, N.J.: Princeton University Press, 1970, p. 466 and ch. 10. On the basis of his study of change in northern Nigeria, Whitaker concludes that the "simple acceptance—displacement hypothesis" that tends to "see confrontation societies as inevitably wracked with strain, conflict, or instability" is too simple. Changing societies can combine modern and traditional elements peacefully.

What, then, have been the major effects of the colonial period on the Nigerian peoples? In the absence of any major commitment to weld a Nigerian identity, differences between the major Nigerian ethnic groups have not decreased. If anything, as the sociologist P. C. Lloyd has indicated, the opposite trend has occurred.

In the present century . . . ease of movement, schooling and a cultural renaissance among the educated elite have tended to produce greater uniformity; for instance, dialects once pronounced, are disappearing. In doing so little to break down traditional patterns of residence and allegiance, economic development had not contributed to any reduction in inter-ethnic differences. In fact, it may be notoriously uneven, and these new inequalities are superimposed on all existing rivalries.[10]

In sum, colonial rule failed to mold all Nigerians into one economic or constitutional system. Therefore, no basis for a dominant set of political attitudes and ethics was created. In fact, the economic and social changes that did occur stimulated the forging of subnational identities in Southern Nigeria where they had been previously weak. Before European rule, the Yoruba were divided among themselves, and so were the Ibo. But with the two groups competing within the same larger system, a common identity developed within each group.

[10] Lloyd, "The Ethnic Background to the Nigerian Crisis," pp. 2, 4.

CHAPTER THREE

The First Republic:
Crises and Collapse

THE NIGERIAN FEDERAL CONSTITUTION OF 1960 was designed to strike the proper balance between regional concerns and central power and to justly represent the federation's minorities. As with any truly federal system, much depended on the patience and compatibility of the participants. The actors in the constitutional drama of 1945–1960—Nigerian and British—were certainly more democratic in their outlook than communist, anarchist, or fascist, yet it is obvious that the governmental system they set up to inaugurate existence as a sovereign state was unable to contain the political style of Nigerians.[1]

When one reviews the events of the 1960s in Africa, it is easy to argue that the "de Gaulle Republic" or the "American quasi-federal system" would have been a more appropriate governmental model than the confederal structure forged for Nigeria. The new African states were by and large unable (or unwilling) to manage the structures bequeathed to them. African leaders regarded fundamental parts of the colonial heritage—regionalization of power, division of executive and legislative roles, independence of the judiciary, judicial review—as subjects for experimentation, and amended constitutions wherever possible.

[1] Surveys of Nigerian constitutional development include Eme O. Awa, *Federal Government in Nigeria*, Berkeley: University of California Press, 1964; Arikpo, *Development of Modern Nigeria* and Ezera, *Constitutional Developments*.

In any event, constitutional modifications did not avert political turmoil, and many African constitutions became historical relics in a series of *coups d'état* after 1965. This chapter describes the mechanics of Nigeria's independence constitution, and the crises faced by the first sovereign government.

The Federal Constitution: Major Provisions

Nigeria began to develop as a federation after the amalgamation of 1914. There never was complete central direction of policy at all levels, but the reasons for federal division were related more to administrative convenience than to intended constitutional decision. After World War II, as the nationalist feeling against British rule grew within a regional context, federation seemed a logical choice as a system that would assuage the mutual fears of the growing Nigerian political elites. As Nigerians themselves participated more fully in constitutional deliberations, powers were increasingly divided up and placed in the hands of regional governments.

By 1960, powers exclusively in the hands of the Federal Government in Lagos were specifically restricted to 44 categories in the areas of fiscal and monetary policy, air and rail transportation, customs, immigration, foreign affairs, and defense. Most important besides these operational powers was the "state of emergency," which the Federal Government could employ to exercise control over a region in case of war, public emergency, or subversion. Other powers, labeled "concurrent," were held mutually by federal and regional governments. One interesting provision in the area of concurrent powers was that in case of conflict between a regional and a federal law, the latter would prevail.

The remaining enumerated powers, concerning law and order, social, and educational questions, were given to the regional governments. Regional police commissions controlled their units and were subject to the federal Police Inspector-General's command, which naturally served to enhance the federal Prime Minister's strength.

All three regional governments were endowed with "incidental" powers to allow them to exercise their specific constitutional prerogatives, a provision similar to the one that gives the American federal government the power to make all laws that are "necessary and proper" to carry out its specified roles. In Nigeria, residual powers not specified in the constitution were handed over to regional governments, as provided by the U.S. Constitution's Tenth Amendment. On these points, Nigeria's constitution contained none of the ambiguities inherent in our own that have fed our "states' rights" controversy during decades of increasing federal responsibilities. As we shall see, however, the specific emergency powers did provide sufficient means for controlling the center of the system. Other constitutional provisions guaranteed human rights and basic freedoms, and barred political pressure against the judiciary and civil services, but by 1965 these appeared insignificant alongside the Federal Government's concerted use of emergency powers. The regions had been soundly defeated even within a constitution designed to preserve them.

Financing the federation proved a thorny issue and clearly demonstrated the desire for power of each of the regions. There were two theoretical alternatives: to budget for the regions in response to their needs or according to the percentage of total revenues which they provided (derivation). Nigerians from the richer Western and Northern Regions advocated the greater use of "derivation." The Eastern Region politicians by and large resisted this trend, at least until after the constitutional shape of Nigeria had been confirmed. Only with large discoveries of oil in the East beginning in the late 1950s did the Easterners begin to prefer derivation.

Provisions for constitutional amendments and machinery for the creation of new states derived from the "rigid" nature of the Nigerian document. The regions did not have the power to initiate an amendment; their role was limited to considering the amendment measures introduced at the federal level. The same "rigid" procedures prevailed in the creation of new regions (or states—the terms were used interchangeably at the time). Federal Legislature began the process with a two-thirds vote in each

House, whereupon existing regional legislatures considered the proposal. Quite clearly, the framers wished to discourage fragmentation of regions, as a majority in the legislature of any . region (or regions) affected by the proposal had to agree. In the first test of this provision, the Western Region Legislature did not support the creation of Midwest State. Events recounted later in this chapter will show why both Western Region resistance and constitutional rigidity were fruitless.

The federal constitution, perfected from 1954 until independence, reflected compromise between major tribes, each of which was assured control over the everyday functions of government in the Region it dominated. In addition there were assurances for Nigeria's smaller minority tribes that their rights would not be violated. For example, the last step in making a new state was a plebiscite among the ethnic groups concerned. There were obvious potential difficulties; provisions would have to be tested to see whether the constitution would actually operate according to expectations. The questionable provisions were mostly intended as centripetal checks on Nigeria's obvious centrifugal tendencies. The framers hoped that, on the one hand, emergency powers for the Federal Government, plus federal predominance in case of conflict between regional and federal laws, would counter any extreme malpractice by the regional governments. Secondly, they assumed that the major ethnic power groups would be content to control their own regions rather than try to take over the federation.

The functions of the Federal Supreme Court included judicial review: Laws and actions could be declared unconstitutional on both regional and federal levels. Obviously, much depended on the judicial system as interpreter of the constitution, as well as protector of the minorities. Initially, the constitutional powers of the judiciary seemed sufficient for its tasks. However, as any student of American democracy realizes, the court's powers are meaningful only when they have been established and accepted by the people through their politicians. It is no accident that, as events of independent Nigeria's first 5 years unfolded, the judiciary was altered more than any other single governmental structure.

This ends a summary of the major aspects of the constitution. A detailed description of governmental structures in the constitution follows.

The Federal Executive

European executive systems tend to confuse Americans accustomed to a political executive who is also head of state. Since many new African states adopted the European model, a discussion of the features will alleviate the confusion.

While the American political executive concentrates power and symbolic features in one office, the British system divides these functions between the Prime Minister and the Crown. The European "divided executive" has one theoretical advantage: The symbolic head of state can remain a useful emotional rallying point even during times when the Prime Minister and his policies are under vicious attack. Conversely, the power of the American executive is strengthened by the symbolic importance of his office.

There is an even more important reason to be concerned with this distinction. Building a nation from diversity will require symbols that can unite people through common aspiration and shared experiences, a fact that many of the Nigerian elite have been aware of. However, tracing the progress of measures to overcome Nigeria's diversity gives the impression that Nigerian politicians were more concerned with preserving their traditional power base within their own region than with creating a firm Nigerian national identity.

When Britain's African colonies became independent, a variation of the British system was introduced. The Queen of England was Nigeria's Head of State, as she was of other Commonwealth countries. After independence, the Queen's Governor-General continued to represent the throne in Nigeria. The title smacked of

British colonial overrule, but during the 1950s real executive power had come under the majority party or coalition in the federal legislature, whose leader was officially titled "Prime Minister" in 1957. Decisions dealing with domestic problems after 1958, and with foreign relations from early in 1960, were made by the Prime Minister and his Council of Ministers. The formal procedures of signing bills into law, and of carrying out "state functions," were included in the largely ceremonial office of Governor-General.

During the colonial era, of course, the governor exercised great power in conjunction with and subject to the authority of British government. Until 1954, the governor steered the legislative process and was its final authority, taking any actions he deemed necessary to maintain order or promote progress, and acting as the administrative head of all public services. He could also make appointments to the legislature, and designate its leader. The governor's control over regional legislation and public services, and his power to dissolve regional legislatures were abrogated in 1954.

In any case, though the British Queen remained the formal head of state, her local representative (the Governor-General) was a Nigerian. Independence brought the transfer of all the Governor-General's real executive powers to the Council of Ministers. The only powers he retained were the rights (1) to be kept informed on public questions by summoning the Prime Minister; (2) to pardon criminals, and (3) to create federal offices and appoint the officeholders. In employing these powers, the Governor-General was to act on the advice of the British government (much like the present British monarch).

The Parliamentary Executive

The functioning governmental executive was the Council of Ministers, headed by the Prime Minister and modeled after the British Cabinet. Two features of the Federal Prime Minister's office jeopardized the operation of the Council of Ministers. In the first place, the office was new and had not had time to prove itself. Regional Premiers took office in 1954, but not until the 1957 constitutional revision was a Federal Prime Minister installed. On Independence Day in 1960, many of the Governor-General's powers were placed in the federal Prime Minister's hands, including presiding over meetings of the Council of Ministers, but regional Premiers had held such power in their own regions since 1958.

Second, and more significant, was the politically inferior nature of the Federal Executive. Well before the 1959 elections, the heads of the 3 major political parties had decided to strengthen their hold in their own regions, each by controlling his own regional legislature. There were two reasons for this decision: to give the party a protected power base and to insure control over legislation and administration in regional government. The extensive functional powers wielded by the regional governments made this control a prerequisite for dispensing patronage. Thus the elected Northern People's Congress (NPC) plurality in the Federal Parliament was not led by Ahmadu Bello, but by his deputy in the NPC, Sir Abubakar Balewa. Likewise, Michael Okpara, Azikwe's successor as leader of the East's National Congress of Nigerian Citizens, remained in his region as Premier. Only in the West did the party leader, Obafemi Awolowo, decide to entrust regional government to his lieutenant. Awolowo, who went to Lagos to lead the opposition in the Federal Legislature, was to regret this move. Chief Samuel Akintola, building his own power base through the great patronage potential in the office of regional Premier, was soon able to contest Awolowo's party control.

The Legislature

The system of apportioning members to the federal House of Representatives faced new problems after 1954, though it had been theoretically improved by direct election. The worst difficulty, to use the language of American malapportionment cases, was that Nigerians in various districts had grossly unequal access to each legislator (see Table 2). Also, some northern constituencies were so large that campaigning was nearly impossible. Finally, because the Lyttleton Constitution had devolved many powers to the regions, control over boundaries of electoral districts was given to regional governments. Obvious gerrymandering possibilities were now under the control of the three political power centers.

Because districts were equalized after 1957 on the basis of approximately one single-member constituency per 95,000 people, the North entered the Federal House the last year before independence with an absolute majority. Southern politicians had resisted this trend in 1954 when the North first demanded half the seats, and they obviously abhorred the new distribution to be used for the 1959 election. It was largely to assuage their fears that the Senate was created by the 1957 Constitutional Conference.

The Senate, or Upper House of the Federal Legislature, served for the same period as the House of Representatives, but could not initiate money bills and could only delay nonmoney bills for 6 months. Obviously, this upper house was not designed to lead government business, but rather to redress the imbalance in the federal system caused by the northern control over the House. Equalizing the constituencies did result in more equitable representation, but jeopardized one of the main conditions of successful federation: symmetry.[2] In the absence of a clearly dominant region with an obviously centralist-oriented leader (a Bismarck-Prussia situation) Nigeria would have been better off with many smaller states more clearly dependent on mutual association and cooperation.

The federal Senate was composed of 54 members: 10 from the Council of Ministers, 12 senators from each Region, 4 from

[2] See Ivo D. Duchacek, *Comparative Federalism: The Territorial Dimension of Politics*, New York: Holt, Rinehart and Winston, 1970, especially ch. 9.

Table 2. Distribution of Seats in the Federal House of Representatives

	1951	1954	1957	1964
Appointed by governor	6	6		
Ex-officio (includes 3 regional attorney-generals)	6	3 (excludes 3 regional att'y-generals)		
Elected (indirectly by regional legislatures)[a]	136	184 elected directly	320	312
North	68 1/250,000[b] (50%)	92 (50%)	174 1/98,500 (54.4%)	167
West	34 1/184,000	42	62 1/99,000	57
East	34 1/184,000	42	62 1/99,000	70
North Cameroon		6	8 1/94,000	[c]
Lagos		2	3 1/93,000	4
Midwest				14

[a] Many MP's were members of both a regional assembly and the Federal House of Representatives.
[b] This fraction indicates the ratio of legislators to population.
[c] After a UN plebescite in 1961, Northern Cameroon entered Nigeria, while the southern part of the Trust Territory chose to become part of the neighboring Republic of Cameroon. It was at this time that the Ibo dominated National Council of Nigeria and Cameroon (NCNC) changed its name to National Congress of Nigerian Citizens.

Lagos, and 4 appointed by the Governor-General. Like the United States Senate before 1913, this indirectly elected Senate was a legislative house that was subservient to the wishes of each respective regional government. Though the Nigerian constitution stated that regional delegations to the Senate should be representative of all major viewpoints in the region, each delegation was more likely to represent its dominant ethnic unit.

The role of the Federal House of Representatives can probably be best understood by observing the regional apportionment of seats that prevailed under various provisions, as shown in Table 2. Much argument accompanied the decision to allocate more seats to the Northern Region in the 1957 constitutional revisions. Southern politicians vociferously pointed out that the preponderant northern population was not a correct indication of northern voting strength deserving representation, because Islam-influenced electoral law withheld the franchise from northern women.

The Judiciary

As one of the basic safeguards for minorities and for the smaller regions, the judicial system of independent Nigeria was obviously a crucial part of the federal machinery. The Supreme Court was intended to act as moderator between the regional and federal governments, preserving the balances set down by the constitution. A second function was also anticipated. As with legislative and executive structures, 1954 had seen the regionalization of the court system. Regional (and Lagos) High Courts were designed to be final arbiters in the majority of cases. Muslim legal concepts worked after 1954 to give northern criminal and civil law a distinct flavor, but the potential of the Federal Supreme Court as a unifier of legal concepts and practices among the regions was strengthened by its appellate function.

Finally, the Independence Constitution did not exclude the right, at that time still in existence in many Commonwealth constitutions, of final appeal to the Judiciary Committee of the Privy Council in England. Thus the ironic situation existed that while Britain had no system of appeal on questions of constitutional interpretation, Nigerians could appeal against the acts of their government to a "higher" authority in England.

Politics in the First Federal Republic

A brief review of the short, anguished history of Nigeria's first independent government offers the best possible insight into the difficulties of operating a democratic governmental system in a setting where democratic values are not yet firmly established. To be sure, there were some positive achievements during Nigeria's first 5 years, especially in the area of foreign affairs, but most accomplishments were destroyed by the chaos and civil war which followed. Nigeria has indeed experienced a decade of crises.[3]

At first, the unity of purpose that appeared to weld Nigerian politicians together after 1954 continued. The mutual enemy—British reluctance to hand over controls as rapidly as Nigerians wished—had been defeated. Several matters briefly took its place as mutual concerns of all Nigerian leaders. Independence was won, and had to be celebrated in a fashion befitting Nigeria's relative standing. Larger than a combination of all the other French and English-speaking West African countries to have become independent that year, Nigeria spent a proportional sum on the celebration. As soon as the fun ended, concerns arose over the slow pace of "Africanization," or replacement of British expatriates in government offices by Nigerians. However, as debate over postindependence relations with Britain intensified, cracks in the foundation of unity appeared.

There were perhaps two reasons why Obafemi Awolowo, from the Western Region and leader of the opposition in the Federal Parliament, sought to make an issue over what he viewed as British strong-arm tactics in forcing Nigeria to sign a defense

---

[3] Fuller accounts of the First Republic are found in Walter Schwarz, *Nigeria*, New York: Praeger, 1968, especially ch. 5–7, and John P. Mackintosh, ed., *Nigerian Government and Politics: Prelude to the Revolution*, Evanston, Ill.: Northwestern University Press, 1966.

agreement. First, he was sincerely concerned about Nigeria's "loss of face" and the consequent weakening of her role as a leader of African nationalism. Second, he wished to begin real opposition to the government. Awolowo's claim that Britain had extracted the use of bases, overflight rights, and tropical training facilities by threatening to delay Nigeria's independence is retrospectively important, because he successfully demonstrated that a working legislative opposition existed. Under Awolowo's prodding, many voices were heard condemning the Defense Pact, which was abrogated in December 1962.

The northern leadership would have had a hard time ignoring Awolowo's political significance. The course of events from mid-1962 until 1966 was related to this first debate, which convinced those in command of the federal policy-making machinery that Awolowo was "dangerous." Several connecting threads can be seen in what followed: First, the power of the northern-dominated coalition came to monopolize the federal system, subduing any potential opposition in the executive and legislative areas. Second, constitutional safeguards, such as the judiciary's role, were ignored. Third, democratic sentiment among Nigerians, tenuous enough to begin with, was further eroded by the events themselves.

Western Region Crisis

While Awolowo was busy leading the federal opposition against the government of Federal Prime Minister Sir Abubakar Balewa of the Northern Peoples Congress, the Western Region's Premier, Chief Akintola, Awolowo's deputy in the Action Group (AG), was strengthening his own political base among the Yoruba. Akintola, a clever politician in his own right, had come to believe by early 1962 that AG ought to try to cooperate with the NPC leaders and join with them in a "National Government." Akintola saw several advantages in such a policy, and was backed by many Yoruba chiefs and by the most important AG financial supporters. Electoral competition in each region since 1959 had sapped the AG treasury, and Akintola saw wisdom in a bargain with NPC in which obvious federal hegemony by the latter would be counter-balanced by promises to recognize AG dominance of Western Region politics and continued control over the midwest. AG could then save money by not continuing the fruitless quest for legislative seats outside the Western Region.

To Awolowo on the other hand, cooperating with NPC for any purpose was now anathema. Supported by AG intelligentsia and those Yoruba masses not closely controlled by traditional chiefs, Awolowo confronted Akintola in the executive meeting of AG early in 1962. This squabble within the top AG leadership was exacerbated by other matters as well. Though both Yoruba, Akintola and Awolowo were from Ijebu and Oyo respectively and their wives were enemies. Finally, Awolowo objected generally to Akintola's conservative political and economic ideas while Akintola saw the AG president as being excessively influenced by extreme left-wingers. This quarrel split the AG, and opened the door to the destruction of opposition within the Federal Parliament.

Having been removed from the office of vice-chairman of AG, Akintola was stripped of the premiership by vote of the back-benchers when the Western Region government tried to convene. Akintola then filed suit against the deposition. Meanwhile, when Chief Adegbenro, the successor for Akintola designated by Awolowo, attempted to convene his new government, the minority of members who were against Awolowo's scheme disrupted the Western Legislature. The majority, 65–52, clearly supported Adegbenro's forming a new government to replace Akintola, and asked the Federal Prime Minister Balewa, to ensure peace in the regional legislature so that the new Western Region government could meet to carry out its business. Balewa refused to promise such protection, and Nigerians were treated during the second year of their independence to the following spectacle in the legislature of the Western Region:

In Ibadan, Alhaji Adegbenro and the Speaker agreed to try once again to hold a meeting some two and a half hours after the first had been disbanded. Policemen were stationed beside and behind the Speaker's Chair. At once, the Akintola faction and the NCNC opposition began to shout and bang their chairs. Chief S. A. Tinuba sat on the floor beside the Speaker's Chair and continually rang a bell. Mr. J. O. Adigun threatened to throw the Record Book at the Speaker. Mr. Akinyemi smashed one despatch box, and Mr. Adedigba threw the other at Alhaji Adegbenro (it was caught by the Sergeant-at-arms). Mr. Adeniya then hit the Speaker with a chair, while the NCNC members smashed theirs or threw them at opponents. All this time the police had been begging the Speaker to let them act, and when he finally did so they again released gas and cleared the House.[4]

On May 29, the Federal Parliament declared a state of emergency, causing the virtual dismemberment of the Western Region government, and the detention by the new "Administrator of Western Region" of all the politicians involved.

The apparent partiality of the federal government was a crucial aspect of these events. Regardless of what may have been the hidden causes of Balewa's actions, the events gave many Nigerians the impression that AG's internal troubles were being used to ensure the end of the troublesome Awolowo. By preventing the intervention of federal police units to ensure order in the Western Region Parliament, Balewa had shown little interest in allowing the western politicians to iron out their difficulties through the accepted procedure of a parliamentary no-confidence vote. Other subsequent actions by the federal government, and by the Administrator appointed to restore order, confirmed the view of millions of Awolowo's supporters that their influence was being systematically destroyed. Six months after the emergency began, Chief Akintola, the exponent of cooperation with Balewa's federal government, had been invited to form a government for Western Region. Awolowo found himself facing the charges of a commission examining the malpractice of Action Group, and then a trial ending in a 10-year sentence for treason.

One clear lesson of the Western Region Crisis was the willingness of the NPC-coalition Federal Government to exercise influence within a region's political affairs in order to ensure a government friendly to NPC aims. The discussion of political

---

[4] John P. Mackintosh, "The Action Group: The Crisis of 1962 and its Aftermath," in Mackintosh, ed., *Nigerian Government*, p. 449.

attitudes in Chapter Five will elucidate some quite understandable reasons for Balewa's willingness to act in this manner in the interests of national unity as he conceived it. Here we must concentrate on the structural changes wrought by actions surrounding the Western Region Crisis. None of those is more important than the impact on the judiciary.

Akintola had filed an action in the Western Region High Court against his dismissal by the regional governor, contending that the governor had no right to decide merely because a majority of the legislative members had signed a petition supporting Adegbenro. The High Court Chief Justice passed Akintola's challenge on to the Federal Supreme Court without ruling, and that Court supported Akintola's claim. At the urging of Awolowo's supporters, however, the Privy Council's Judiciary Committee considered the dispute and reversed the Nigerian Federal Supreme Court's decision in May 1963. Though Awolowo's followers were heartened by this outcome, it was ignored by the federal government, and resulted in one of the significant constitutional changes that was to follow.

Republican Constitution, 1963

By 1963, Balewa's government had begun to tie together its thoughts on the ills of the Independence Constitution. At the Federal Prime Minister's initiative, a conference was called in Lagos to be attended by politicians of all viewpoints (except for those who were restricted to their homes, or in jail). The most publicized change agreed on by the conference was the creation of a Republic. In simple terms, this involved the transfer of the role of Governor-General as surrogate head-of-state (acting on behalf of the English Queen) to an indirectly elected president who would serve 5 years. Except for its symbolic significance, to be treated in Chapter Five, this move was of far less consequence than other results of the conference. The Republican Constitution fully demonstrated Balewa's desire to strengthen the hand of northern-led coalition by increasing the power of the parliamentary executive (Council of Ministers) while limiting the roles of head of state and judiciary.

In spite of the protests by Nnamdi Azikiwe, already the Governor-General and likely to be chosen by the Federal Parliament as Nigeria's first president, the chief of state's powers were reduced. Azikiwe's view was that the office's executive role should be expanded. The NPC leaders argued that such a change would obviously give northerners control of the office. In the final document the presidency lost ground; ambiguities that had previously appeared to give the Governor-General some area for initiative in removing the prime minister were replaced by a firm statement that the prime minister could be dismissed only through a no-confidence vote in Parliament.

The legislature's ability to hinder action by the Cabinet was also reduced. The new Republican Constitution provided that if the government drew a vote of no-confidence and was forced to resign, the Parliament would also be dissolved! Most members objected during debate to this provision, seeing it as a threat to their freedom to debate. How many government backbenchers were likely to join a protest against their Cabinet if they knew that every no-confidence vote would force them to contest a new election?

The legal realm witnessed the most serious changes brought about by the Republican Constitution. A decision made earlier to abolish final appeals to the Privy Council in London was formally included, making the Nigerian Federal Supreme Court the highest court of appeal. More important, after long argument the Judicial Services Commission was abolished, giving the Federal Prime Minister power over judicial appointments. A third procedural change in the area of law was attempted, but the provisions of the Preventive Detention Act failed because of popular opposition.

These changes in judicial procedure certainly imposed very serious limits on the power and independence of Nigeria's courts. Besides the constraints placed on the prospects for impartial justice, a detrimental, longterm blow was dealt to the Court's major but intangible role as final arbiter in constitutional matters.

As American students well know, one of the Supreme Court's major functions is to interpret our laws and constitution for the understanding of the citizenry. *Miranda v. Arizona* is more important for the principle than for the individuals involved in the specific case. Especially in a new country, where the practices of fair government need public specification, the educative role of a free court system is crucial. Changes in the Nigerian judiciary were unquestionably headed in the direction of limiting this important function.[5]

The decennial census in 1962 unfortunately overlapped with these events. A census usually has political overtones, and in Nigeria's case the census was laden with political dynamite. Emotions reached a climax in February 1964. For years southern Nigerians had harbored deep suspicions that the North's population was much smaller than it had claimed in the 1952-1953 census (see Table 3). These earlier population figures had proven of great significance: Northern dominance of the Federal House of Representatives was based on them. The first results of the 1962 census showed a radically decreased proportion of Nigeria's population living in the Northern Region. The imbalance had shifted from 57 percent in favor of the North in 1952 to a 49 percent minority in 1962. After the 1962 census had been rejected by

Table 3.   Population Figures (in millions)

	1952–1953 census	1962 census	1962 (revised)	1963 (revised)
North	16.8	22.5	31.0	29.8
East	7.2	12.4	12.3	12.4
West	4.6	7.8	7.8	10.3
Midwest	1.5	2.2	2.2	2.5
Lagos	0.3	0.7	0.7	0.7
Total	30.4	45.6	54.0	55.7

SOURCE: Walter Schwarz, *Nigeria*, New York: Praeger, 1968, p. 163.

[5] On judicial development in the First Republic, see Paul O. Proehl, "Fundamental Rights Under the Nigerian Constitution, 1960–1965," Los Angeles: University of California, African Studies Center, *Occasional Paper* #8.

northern leaders, there were vast migrations of tribesmen back to their "home" regions. Entire "new villages" were discovered, especially in Iboland, and the census turned into a political exercise. Obviously, southern Nigerians were determined to wrest power from the Hausa-Fulani by manipulating the results. The federal government forestalled this by condemning the 1962 census and revising the figures. The subsequent southern outcry led to a completely new census in late 1963. The results published in February 1964, showing a majority retained by the northerners, were rejected by the leader of the National Congress of Nigerian Citizens, Dr. Michael Okpara.[6]

Divided by the Western Region Crisis, the Preventive Detention Act, the census dispute, and other lesser arguments, Nigerians were becoming more disillusioned each month. Development and rising incomes were not on the scale that the masses had hoped for and had been promised. Politicians, in their interminable quest for more wealth and power, were disappointed by each other, and the educated elite was perhaps the most bitter of all, as this statement by Odili, the intellectual in Achebe's novel, A Man of the People, shows:

> What would happen if I were to push my way to the front and up the palm-leaf-festooned dais, wrench the microphone from the greasy hands of that babbling buffoon and tell the whole people—this vast contemptible crowd—that the great man they had come to hear with their drums and dancing was an honorable Thief. But of course they knew that already. No single man and woman there that afternoon was a stranger to that news. . . . And because they all knew, if I were to march up to the dais now and announce it they would simply laugh at me and say: What a fool![7]

While the NPC leaders had achieved apparent success in gaining control of the central and regional governments of the federation, events had destroyed the hopes of many Nigerians

[6] Nigerian population growth is discussed in Schwarz, Nigeria, pp. 157–164, and in Étienne Van de Walle, "Who's Who and Where in Nigeria," Africa Report 15, no. 1 (January, 1970): 22–23.

[7] Chinua Achebe, A Man of the People, New York: John Day, 1966, pp. 130–131. Copyright © 1966 by Chinua Achebe. Reprinted by permission of The John Day Company, Inc., publisher, and William Heinemann Ltd.

that independence would bring democracy and development. Some of these frustrations surfaced in the General Strike of 1964. To cement Nigeria's faction-ridden labor movement into concerted action required unique conditions. These were supplied by the government's lack of sympathy with the recommendations of a commission that had found the minimum wage for government employees to be less than half what was required to meet the cost-of-living expenses in Lagos for a family of four. Nigerians were becoming increasingly aware of the fantastic wage differences in their country. "The ratio between the earnings of a messenger and those of a permanent secretary, between 1:30 or 1:40 in Nigeria, is about 1:12 in Britain and about 1:15 in the United States." [8] Nigeria's labor leaders, frustrated for years by the divisions in their ranks, were finally able to mobilize their own members. They also derived sympathy and support from people outside the labor movement and succeeded in paralyzing Nigeria during early June 1964. More importantly, attention had been focused on the corruption, lack of development, and ineffectiveness of Nigeria's first independent regime.

These political wars led to a rearrangement of Nigeria's political party coalitions. In 1964, the main contestants gathered for what was to be the last major event of Nigeria's short period of democratic experiment. New political party alignments were creating the very situation most feared by northern leaders. Up to that time, the Ibo-dominated NCNC had served as junior partners in the federal coalition, whose main victims had been Awolowo and his Yoruba followers. Now the census fiasco convinced Okpara that alliance with the Hausa-Fulani was untenable. Angered by Akintola's support of the revised 1964 census results (an issue which should have united all southerners) Okpara influenced NCNC participants in Akintola's Western Region government to leave the regional coalition. Okpara's NCNC then formed the United Progressive Grand Alliance (UPGA) consisting of NCNC, Awolowo's AG, and northern minority and opposition parties. The sole basis of this alliance was anti-northern feeling. The

[8] Schwarz, *Nigeria*, p. 25.

UPGA confronted a new coalition, the Nigeria National Alliance (NNA) headed by NPC and including Akintola's segment of Yoruba, then known as Nigerian National Democratic Party (NNDP), plus several other small southern parties opposed to NCNC.

Elections which occasioned these plans and alliances were to be held on the federal level in December 1964, and in Western Region a year later. At first, UPGA anticipated victory, if electoral malpractice could be kept down. But as UPGA affiliates controlled only two of the four regional governments (the East and Midwest) and victory in all three southern regions was a requisite for ousting the northerners from control of the Federal Government, there was a reason to be anxious. After observing several real and imagined abuses, UPGA ordered a boycott of the elections. Because the regional governments were responsible for electoral machinery in their regions, the UPGA boycott was successfully carried out in most of their constituencies. In March 1965, the federal government held elections in those regions in spite of the boycott, but the UPGA leaders had successfully undercut any emotional support which might have been awarded the victors.

Both the Yoruba and Ibo grew progressively more sullen during these events. The undermining of public confidence in the motives of the federal government was completed by the regional election which followed in the West. NNDP victory, owing heavily to the ability of the despised Akintola government to manipulate electoral machinery, combined with falling cocoa prices to produce virtual chaos there by the year's end. By December 1965, Nigeria was on the brink of collapse.

CHAPTER FOUR

Nigerian Military
Government Since 1966

NIGERIA WAS ONE of many African countries subjected to army intervention after June 1965, when a coup in Algeria seemed to open a floodgate of political action by African military organizations. Ironically, during the first few years of African independence, political scientists generally viewed the small armies as politically insignificant, concentrating instead on such topics as charismatic leadership and single-party systems. Few political analysts were concerned that Africa might begin a "Latin American period" of army rule.

Conditions that Brought the Coup

Needless to say, the various coups were followed by a torrent of analyses of the conditions within African armies, and of the probable cause for their sudden political role.[1] Most accounts refer to two fundamental causes: decay of the political system, and especially the political parties, and growing perception by the

---

[1] Good general analyses are Claude E. Welch, Jr., *Soldier and State in Africa*, Evanston, Ill.: Northwestern University Press, 1970, ch. 1, Aristide Zolberg, *Creating Political Order; the Party States of West Africa*, Chicago: Rand McNally, 1966, and especially J. J. Miners, *The Nigerian Army 1956-1966*, London: Methuen, 1971.

army of its possible political influence. Both elements were present in the case of Nigeria by 1966.

DECAY OF THE POLITICAL SYSTEM

In African and Asian countries that were dominated by a single nationalist political organization, postindependence euphoria tended to hide a process which boded ill for the future. With its principal function complete, party machinery decayed as the middle- and lower-level cadres began to enjoy the fruits of their victory. Many sought jobs in the bureaucracy. The challenge of governing the new state, which included carrying out the omnipresent "development plan," overshadowed the preindependence concern for mobilizing mass support. The inevitable result was a growing gulf between leaders (Nkrumah and Sukarno, for example) and their popular mass power base. Dominant, charismatic leaders could try to offset this trend by increasing their direct appeal to the masses, thereby bypassing the decaying intermediate party machinery. Nkrumah became the "redeemer" while Sukarno proposed vast, impossible coalitions among his diverse peoples. Both leaders employed propaganda slogans to promote emotional commitment. More perceptively, Nyerere of Tanganyika decided to attack the problem directly by "rebuilding the party."

Nigeria's political decay took a different form. As a multiparty system, at least on the federal level, it was less likely that competing Nigerian leaders would allow their party machines to decompose. On the contrary, from 1959 until the army coups ended political organization, Nigeria's parties became more efficient. Determined to dominate at least their own region, each party mobilized for electoral warfare of extraordinary brutality. The excesses of this turmoil led governmental leaders to believe that force would be necessary to ensure the continued operation of basic services in certain areas of the country.

Political scientists generally agree that stable politics depends on some combination of mutual satisfaction felt by participants within the system and legitimate use of force. However, there has not been enough analysis of the conditions that produce instability, cases where force is likely to take over from voluntary compliance. The sociologist Talcott Parsons has described these settings as "power deflations" which lead inevitably to the use of force as a substitute.[2] In the Nigerian case, "power deflation" included the intensifying of ethnic conflict, some awareness and deepening of social tensions, gross electoral manipulations, growing internal crime and violence, disillusionment among intelligentsia, and increased reliance on the state's oppressive machinery to keep the peace. Some of these economic, social, and political conditions are treated in detail elsewhere (especially Chapter Eight), but their relationship to developments within the military will be clarified in this chapter.

THE NIGERIAN ARMY BECOMES POLITICAL

With conditions leading the political elite toward an increasing reliance on force, the values and outlook of Nigerian soldiers toward politics began to change from those of the colonial era. It is important to emphasize the apolitical heritage of the Nigerian military, a fact that helps explain the ambivalence of officers in English-speaking African countries when they began to perceive that they were the only alternative to corruption and chaos. They had always been clearly instructed that soldiers are to obey politicians. Anthony Sampson has described British civil–military relations:

> Politicians remain firmly in control of the services. Britain has never had a separate fighting caste . . . most service chiefs have (in contrast to Americans) remained part of a broader society . . . they have never had the chance to develop folie de grandeur, and they have become used to being cut down and bullied by politicians in peacetime. . . . "It's a kind of a miracle in Europe," said an African leader after the mutinies of 1964, "that the armies take orders from civilians."[3]

Statements of the majors who carried out the Janauary 1966 coup demonstrate beyond doubt their deep concern with reforming Nigerian life. Because politicians were at the center of the

[2] Cited in Welch, *Soldier and State*, p. 22.
[3] Anthony Sampson, *The Anatomy of Britain Today*, New York: Harper & Row, 1965, pp. 365–366.

corruption and cynicism, officers decided that "politicians must go"—a recurring theme in African and Asian coups. When officers conclude that civilian rule is contradictory to the country's development, the "disposition to intervene" appears. Major Nzeogwu, the coordinator of the January coup, states: "Our purpose was to change our country." [4] This "disposition to intervene" was nourished by the increasing frequency of military action: Coups in Dahomey, Central African Republic, and Upper Volta immediately preceded similar events in Nigeria and Ghana. Contagion is frequently cited as a factor contributing to military intervention.

A second condition for political action by the army was the passive response of the former European power. By 1966, African officers' growing concern for the welfare of their countries was buttressed by the knowledge that France, England, and Belgium seemed interested in reacting only when specifically invited by a strong civilian regime popular enough to resist the initial efforts of a coup or mutiny (Tanganyika, Kenya, and Uganda in 1964). Coups which had appeared to be popular, and/or were sufficiently unforeseen and irrevocable, had not brought European response (Gabon, Congo-Brazzaville, Togo, Central African Republic, Zanzibar, Dahomey).

On the night of January 14-15, 1966, a coup organized by five Nigerian army majors was initiated.[5] Though many of the plans formulated among various sectors of Nigeria's elite may never be known, there were indications that the northern politicians were planning a move which would strengthen their control over the entire federal system. Some of the key participants in meetings held in January 1966 were subsequently killed, and the exact context of the coup that did occur is unclear. In any case, the Northern and Western regional capitals of Kaduna and Ibadan were successfully taken over by the plotters, but their failure in the federal capital led to their eventual downfall. In Lagos, commanding General Ironsi escaped to the barracks outside the city

---

[4] Recounted in Schwarz, Nigeria, p. 191.
[5] Accounts of the 1966 events are found in Ibid., ch. 8, and in Panter-Brick, ed., Nigerian Politics and Military Rule.

and took over the garrison, bringing order to Lagos and then Ibadan. By afternoon on January 15, garrisons in Enugu and Benin had been contacted by Ironsi and had sworn allegiance to him. However, Major Nzeogwu and his troops were traveling south from Kaduna, apparently in a move on Ibadan and Lagos to reverse the coup's sagging fortunes.

While Nzeogwu moved south, what remained of the Federal Council of Ministers struggled to designate a deputy prime minister who could give orders to the loyal troops under Ironsi. Faced with their indecision, Ironsi indicated to the Cabinet that, in order to ensure the obedience of his troops, it would be necessary for him to take command. With Ironsi newly invested as "Head of the Federal Military Government and Supreme Commander of the Nigerian Armed Forces," Nzeogwu and the other coup leaders gave up and were detained in Lagos. As one British journalist wrote.

It had been a dream of a coup. "Bang, bang, you're dead!"—a satisfying infantile aggression fantasy. In a single night the Sardauna of Sokoto, symbol of Hausa-Fulani domination and of feudalistic reaction, Chief Akintola, high priest of election rigging, and Chief Okotie-Eboh, byword for luxury and ministerial corruption, had been killed.[6]

At first the coup was welcomed, even in the North. Though an Ibo, Ironsi had been appointed Commanding General by the northerner Balewa a year before and Head of the Federal Military by a northerner-dominated Cabinet. Nor did the army at that time appear as concerned with tribal jealousies as did the other sectors of Nigerian life. January's happenings appeared to many Nigerians to be an "Ibo coup." The army majors involved have insisted that it was not, stressing that their plans merely failed in Eastern Region before Okpara could be added to the list of assassinated regional prime ministers. That an Ibo, Ironsi, had emerged from the turmoil in charge was coincidental. In February 1965, the Federal Prime Minister, a Fulani, had picked Ironsi, the only Ibo among Nigeria's four major-generals, as Army Chief-of-Staff.

[6] *Ibid.*, pp. 198–199.

Ironsi demonstrated little political ability in making the most of the unique consensus that temporarily existed among Nigerians. His position was perhaps impossible in any event. Southerners saw the detained army majors as heroes; though upset by the assassinations of Sir Ahmadu Bello, spiritual as well as political leader of the North, and of several ranking northern military personnel. Northerners did not generally want the old system reconstructed, but they did want to see the mutineers tried for the murder of their officers. Ironsi might have compromised these two demands, but no apparent attempt was even made. One good move was to appoint Major Hassan Katsina, a northerner, as Northern Military Governor. Ironsi proved less perceptive by appointing an Ibo to investivate the prospects for rapid unification of the civil services! Since control over the regional civil service was cherished by northerners as a safeguard against Ibo infiltration and domination, Ironsi's decision was not welcomed.

From the coup until May, Ironsi's regime steadily deemphasized Nigeria's long-standing regional divisions and tried to create a strong unitary state. However, popular support for some of the government's moves, such as investigations into corruption of politicians, was undermined by sudden accumulations of wealth by elements of the army officer corps. Finally, and the most important factor in his loss of popular support was Ironsi's haste in proclaiming a new Unitary Constitution (Decree #34, May 24, 1966) even before the commissions directed to study a new constitutional arrangement could turn in their reports.

Riots in the northern cities were a direct consequence of Decree #34. Demonstrators called for a referendum on that decree; failing that, they demanded secession. The riots quickly became a pogrom against Ibo sectors of northern cities, where an estimated three thousand were killed. The military governors were called to Lagos to discuss the situation with Ironsi and returned to their regions with statements assuring the people that Decree #34 had intended no rapid unification without consulting them. Emirs in the northern cities accepted these assurances, and the military governor of Eastern Region, Colonel Odumegwu Ojukwu, entreated his fellow Ibo to return to their jobs and homes in the North. In an attempt to identify and contend with basic grievances, Ironsi toured the country, departing from his base of power in Lagos, and thereby exposed himself to the second coup.

Leaving aside the question of who caused "round two," the murder of three Ibo officers in a Western Region barracks served to trigger the series of events that reversed Ironsi's rapid centralization of Nigerian government. Northern officers, mostly colonels, killed Ironsi near Ibadan on July 29, 1966. The senior officer surviving Ironsi (whose death was not immediately known) was a Yoruba, Brigadier General Ogundipe. He started out for Lagos to put down the new revolt but was stopped by rebel forces. At this point Ojukwu called Ogundipe, offering him full support if the latter could take over the Supreme Command in Ironsi's absence. Ogundipe was not confident of being obeyed by the northern troops in the area and his vacillations encouraged wild speculation from various quarters—for example, the possibility of secession by the North and West together from the federation. Lieutenant-Colonel Yakubu Gowon, Army Chief of Staff, was sent to talk with the rebels on July 31, and emerged from these discussions as the new Supreme Commander. It seems likely that Gowon (who came from a small non-Moslem northern tribe, the Anga) was accepted by the northern rebels because he agreed with their premise that strong union was impossible. He was acceptable to southerners because he was neither Moslem nor Hausa.

As soon as Gowon had obtained the allegiance of barracks in the West and North, he announced that Nigeria would return to federal structures, and a civilian-dominated convention would be called to formulate the new constitutional provisions. To end the killings within the army, eastern officers and troops were sent home, and northern troops were withdrawn from the East.

Biafran Secession and the Civil War

There were several causes for the next major event in Nigeria's tortured development. In the first place, the regime headed by Gowon was never able to establish sovereignty over the Eastern

Region. Ojukwu had accepted Ironsi's control in January, but denied Gowon's superiority and declared the new federal regime illegal when it took command in July.

A more important reason is the reversal of northern and eastern sentiment towards the degree of regional autonomy the new federal system should have. By September 1966, a conference was convened in Lagos. Northern delegates preferred a confederal system with virtual political autonomy for the regions, including the right to secede, but with a "Common Services Organization" to coordinate mutual concerns such as transportation and telecommunications. Eastern- and Western-Region delegations also offered confederal proposals. Only the Midwest preferred the prospect of continuing the pre-1966 federal system.

At this point, the new controlling military elements, apparently led by Gowon, pressured the northern delegation to reconsider its proposals. A radically revised northern document struck out the "secession clause," reinforced the powers of the federal government, and accepted the concept of smaller regions carved out of the existing four. Northern "minority" military and civilian elements had an important role in this change. Gowon himself came from a small Christian tribe in the "middle belt," the southern fringe of the Northern Region. These minority tribesmen, many of whom served in the Nigerian army, disliked the prospect of increased power for the Hausa-Fulani-dominated Northern Region government. Regardless of whether Gowon and other "minority" elements were responsible for this change in the northern delegation's outlook, watchful Ibo, who dominated the eastern delegation, saw a threat in the creation of more regions, and were on the brink of serious disagreement with the northern delegation.

At this juncture, during September and October 1966, 30,000 Ibo were killed in the North, in a slaughter far beyond the scale of the May riots. Northerners were still incensed at the earlier assassinations of their leadership, and the presence of thousands of Ibo traders, businessmen, and civil servants living in the North presented constant reminder of this communal bitterness. In a sense, this pogrom carried out against Ibo in the North was the crucial turning point away from Nigerian unity. The Ibo always had been "nationally minded," in part because their ambition and modern outlook made them successful in competition with other ethnic groups outside their regions. Facing what they perceived to be a systematic extermination in the North, their confidence in national unity was no longer justified. An analysis of Ojukwu's speeches between August 1966, and March 1967, indicates that he used strongly secessionist symbols beginning on October 5, 1966. Ojukwu's new tone replaced an ambivalent mixture of nationalist and regionalist images prevalent after the May outburst of killings.[7]

Ojukwu's state of mind is noted because of his importance in determining the course of Nigerian events from 1967–1970. Attempts to foster productive dialogue between Ojukwu and the Federal Military Government were doomed to failure after October 1966, because the Eastern Military Governor saw little future for the Ibo within a greater Nigeria. The de facto secession of the Eastern Region dates from October 1966, after which time no effective federal power was exercised there. A series of diplomatic negotiations between Ojukwu and the Federal Government ensued, but civil war ended these endeavors. Few people on either side made any attempt to soften the impact of inflammatory events on ethnic attitudes. In spite of the efforts of the Northern Military Governor, Hassan Katsina, to convince the mobs to stop killing easterners during the September–October massacres, there were several reports of army and police leadership in some of the northern gangs.[8] Likewise, Colonel Ojukwu's eastern government made every attempt to publicize the sordid details in order to forge eastern solidarity.

Either because of real fear for his life, or the desire to mold a united easterners' will after the massacres, Ojukwu insisted that

[7] Gary M. Duck, "The Symbols of Political Disintegration in Nigeria: A Content Analysis of Speeches by Lt. Col. Chukwremeka Ojukwu," unpublished paper presented at Rocky Mountain Social Science Association annual meeting, May, 1969.

[8] Frederick Forsyth implicates Northern Nigerian officialdom in the massacres in his pro-Biafran account, The Biafra Story, Baltimore: Penguin, 1969, ch. 6.

steps be taken to ensure his safety if he were to leave his region for discussions with the federal leadership. Accusations by both sides of military equipment purchases also created further tension. The atmosphere for a reconciliation attempt was already cloudy when the government of Ghana arranged to host a discussion between Ojukwu and the federal military leaders in January 1967.

Accounts of this meeting, in Aburi on the outskirts of Ghana's capital city, concur that Ojukwu was the most purposeful, prepared, and tactically clever of the participants. In Ojukwu's view, Gowon and the Federal side supported his hypothesis at the meeting that the regions of Nigeria would have to be separate long enough for emotional wounds to heal before any further hopes of amicable federal cooperation would be justified. To Ojukwu, the Aburi talks had confirmed short-term independence for his region. After heated discussion, there was apparent agreement that there should be regionalization of the army and a wide measure of effective separation "to avoid further friction and further killing." The participants also came to accept Ojukwu's view that the term "Supreme Commander" would overemphasize the position of the Lagos government within the looser association. They substituted "Commander in Chief and Head of the Federal Military Government" in place of the Ironsi-era title. Recruitment of Yoruba was accepted as a means of effecting the last unfinished item of military regionalization. Most important of all, Gowon and his cohorts accepted the Ojukwu formula of no crucial federal decisions without agreement by all regional governors.

Only after they returned to Nigeria did the federal leaders realize the significance of the agreement Ojukwu had extracted from them. They had consented to what they thought were temporary measures, but now perceived that Ojukwu could employ the Aburi provisions to create a virtually separate country. This point was brought home to the military leaders by civil servants, who pointed out that regional agreement on crucial matters, and the transfer of power from Supreme Commander to a Supreme Military Council, would render regional military commanders unassailable.[9]

As the fiscal year drew to a close in March 1967, Ojukwu remained firmly committed to the agreements hc had engineered in Aburi. Sensing that the outwitted federal leaders would now have to disclaim those agreements, Ojukwu steadily prepared the Eastern Region to "go it alone" by retaining funds collected for disbursement at the federal government level. Beginning April 1, Ojukwu intended to be certain that the Eastern Region would be able to pay civil servants who had retreated from other parts of Nigeria after the massacres. It was at that time, also, that intensive efforts were begun to prepare eastern civilians for the possibility of war, stressing the necessity of armed preparedness to counter any federal initiative.

If the federal leaders were instransigent about continuing the federation in spite of the depth of easterners' bitterness, easterners demonstrated a similar degree of obstinancy in the last event of precivil war drama. Federal Decree #8 went as far as Gowon and his supporters could possibly go in the direction of regional power without corroding all the remaining preservatives of unity. Decree #8 receives further treatment below, as it is central to understanding the structure of Nigeria's current governmental system, but it is also significant within this sequence of events. According to Decree #8, the federal government was now willing to follow the Aburi agreement; no crucial decisions would be made without consent of all regional military governors. In spite of this, Ojukwu hastily condemned the decree. Former President Azikiwe has commented that "Ojukwu's greed blinded him to fail to realize the great concessions he had won."[10] Leaving aside the question of Ojukwu's personal ambitions, a more objective assessment must stress the importance of emergency powers, which the federal government intended to retain.

[9] The Aburi discussions and their consequences are recounted in Panter-Brick, ed., *Nigerian Politics and Military Rule*, pp. 35–45.

[10] Namdi Azikiwe, *Origins of the Nigerian Civil War*, Apapa: The Nigerian National Press, 1969, p. 10.

Ojukwu's rejection of Decree #8 coincided with other fast-moving events that nearly divided Nigeria into four parts. Awolowo, released from jail, pointed out that failure to meet Ojukwu's demands fully would be an indication to the Yoruba and other southern peoples that the federal government was uninterested in their feelings. The West, asserted Awolowo, would also consider secession.

At this juncture, the northern leadership of emirs and military officers realized that a major concession was inevitable, and reversed the long-standing northern opposition to "new states." Always jealous of any encroachment into their solidarity, which they saw as essential for protection against inroads of Ibo into their power structure, northern leadership now agreed to the creation of more states. Awolowo was convinced by this that Gowon and his backers meant well, and the popular Yoruba leader withdrew his objections.

Now united in its efforts to reintegrate the Eastern Region through diplomacy, Gowon's government appointed a National Reconciliation Committee, which visited Ojukwu and listened to his viewpoints. Gowon accepted their recommendation to end economic sanctions against the East. In the East, minds were already made up and 10 days after this offer by Gowon, Biafra's secession was announced.

The horrors of Nigeria's civil war have been described elsewhere, and generally lie outside the purview of this book.[11] However, the war's impact on Nigeria today must not be ignored and will be treated in the subsequent chapters on political attitudes, development problems, and foreign relations. Here we are concerned with the impact of the civil war on governmental structure and operation.

The African armies have generally been a force for unity within

[11] The Civil War can be studied in Sir Rex Niven, *The War of Nigerian Unity*, London: Evans, 1970; Anthony Kirk-Greene, *Crisis and Conflict in Nigeria: A Documentary Sourcebook, 1966–1970*, London: Oxford University Press, 1971; John de St. Jorre, *The Nigerian Civil War*, London: Hodder and Stoughton, 1971; and through the nine short stories in *The Insider: Stories of War and Peace from Nigeria*, Enugu: Nwankwo and Ifejika Publishing Co., 1971.

the new countries. The Biafran secession was a rare case in emergent Africa: the first instance where ethnic conflict split the military, usually the most "national" of the new country's institutions. Coincidentally these ethnic divisions corresponded with age-generational levels, and with political leanings and friendships. Most of the highest ranking officers had developed connections with the ruling politicians; Brigadier Ademulegun was friendly with the Sarduna of Sokoto, Brigadier Maimalari with Akintola and other NNDP leaders. The majors who plotted the January coup were mostly Ibo, and were affiliated with various more radical elements among the intelligentsia and civil service. One of their plans, for example, was to install Awolowo as Executive President.[12] Intervention by most African armies was intended to supplant ethnic and political divisions. In Nigeria's case, these tensions fed on military rule.

Structure of the Federal Military Government

Important changes that have been retained in the current Nigerian governmental system include (1) increased influence by political and military leaders of minority tribes at the expense of Ibo, Yoruba, and Hausa-Fulani; (2) replacement of political party leaders by the military as general policy makers; (3) increased policy-making role for permanent secretaries and top echelons of civil service; and (4) replacement of the four powerful regions by twelve "states."

The first of these developments will be discussed at length in Chapters Five and Six, but it cannot be ignored here. Prior to its politicization in 1966, the Nigerian army had been predominantly composed of a curious mixture of minority tribe troops, mostly Tiv and other middle belt northerners, and Ibo officers. The slaughters of July 1966 changed the ethnic texture of the army drastically. Ibo troops and officers were killed or left in the

[12] A. R. Luckham, *The Nigerian Military: A Case Study in Institutional Breakdown*, unpublished doctoral dissertation, Univ. of Chicago, 1969, pp. 160 f.

North; northerners deserted units located in the east. Most units in the Western Region were manned by northerners, since few Yoruba had shown much interest in military life. By March 1967, it was only Ojukwu's East Region that was rebelling against the new Gowon regime. The Midwest Regional Governor, Colonel Ejoor, insisted that his region be completely demilitarized; he feared the Midwest would become a battle zone between the federal government and a secessionist East. Far more serious, Awolowo's Yoruba supporters in the Western Region were chafing against what they perceived as military occupation by the North. Awolowo even hinted that if Ojukwu led the East into secession, the West would not be far behind!

At this crucial point a major concession was produced by a conference of northerners entitled "Leaders of Thought." Without the imposing authority of the Sardauna of Sokoto, assassinated a year before, a trend toward autonomy had emerged among the northern emirs. The views of northern minority tribe leaders and minority elements in the army added to the new sense of localism that prevailed, and explain the surprising call for creation of new states which came from the meeting of the northern "Leaders of Thought." This move was welcomed by Awolowo and the midwestern leadership, and set the stage for his entrance into the Federal Government as Minister of Finance. It also represented a radical departure from the previous structure of Nigerian federation. As revised after May 1967, when twelve states were officially decreed, Nigerian federal government consisted of the structures shown in Table 4.

State and Local Government

Subfederal administrative levels under the military regime reflect the inherent chain of command in a military organization. Modifying this system is the fact that the Federal Military Government is willing to appoint civil servants for the office of Governor, e.g., Ukpapi Asika of East Central State (formerly Biafra). Furthermore, for military men appointed to the post, the door seems open for their development as politicians with a power base, as demonstrated by the action of Kano State Governor Bako in publicly recommending the use of Port Harcourt as a second harbor to lessen dock congestion at Lagos Apapa port.[13] Governor

Table 4.   Organization of the Federal Military Government
(since January 1970)

Organization	Members	Duties
Supreme Military Council (SMC)	Chairman of SMC[a] Heads of Navy and Air Force 12 Governors of States[c]	Supervises all Federal legislative and executive powers[b] Exclusive Federal Powers: Post, Defense, Telecommunications, External Affairs
Federal Executive Council	SMC members Inspector-General of Police Attorney-General 15 Cabinet department heads	Assumed functions of former Council of Ministers
Federal Supreme Court	Chief Justice 3 Associate Justices 12 State Chief Justices	Duties do *not* include judicial review
State Government Executive Councils (12 in all)	Governor Commissioner of Police Chief Law Officer Permanent Secretaries	Administer the affairs of their states
State High Courts State Appeals Courts		

[a]Title changed to "Chairman of SMC" by Constitutional Decree, March 17, 1967. This act ended use of the title "Supreme Commander of the Armed Forces and Head of the Federal Military Government" (created January 17, 1966).
[b]Vested by March 17, 1967 Constitution (Suppression and Modification Decree).
[c]After "12-state decree," May 26, 1967, abolished former four Regions.

[13] *West Africa*, May 1–7, 1971.

Bako has become the advocate for interests in his state. In another example, Benue-Plateau State Governor Gomwalk entered the delicate dispute over Lagos' status, calling for the removal of the federal capital from Lagos State. It is understandable that northerners would prefer to see a more centrally located federal capital, but the prospect of colonels who serve as state governors publicly announcing their own views is certainly enlightening. (Gomwalk later retracted his statement, insisting that he had been misquoted.)[14]

Furthermore disputes between states in Nigeria are not always handled with the hierarchical tendencies of military organization. Rivers and East Central have a running dispute over who owns Rivers State properties, taken from the retreating Ibos during 1968–1970. Public debate finds the Rivers Government refusing to restore property to the former owners without first being given the register of titles and deeds for examination. The federal government may yet arbitrate the matter, but the degree of state initiative is surprising.[15] Given the long-term trend toward increased centralization of power, however, the principal question for state-level government is how much political initiative will be retained at that level.

While state governments are structurally similar to each other, local government in Nigeria retains the variety established during the colonial era. In the six states carved out of the Northern Region in 1967, local government is organized on as many as four levels; from Village Council up through Village Group Council and District Council to the unit still known as "Native Authority" in the Northwestern State and Northeastern State. The inherent strength of this multilevel system is its proximity to the people in their remote, rural communities, enhanced by the presence of traditional chiefs. Kwara State has broken away from the old native authority system to the degree that chiefs no longer sit on that state's Divisional or District Councils, and the number of local government levels has been reduced to two.

[14] West Africa, June 4–11, 1971.
[15] West Africa, April 17–23, 1971.

Generally, in the six northern states authority relationships between local government levels are hierarchical.

In the three states which derived from the Western and Midwestern Regions, there was only one level of local government, the District Council. Two other levels were intended, but over two decades the Divisional Council, superior to the Districts, and the inferior Local Councils, have given up authority and in the majority of cases, disappeared. District Councils have, therefore, taken over a wide variety of functions, including providing basic health services, cemetaries, trash and sewage removal, and maintaining of roads and street lights, and other public works.

In the three eastern states, local government was temporarily superseded by direct state-level administration of areas as they were recaptured from the Biafran insurgents.

Two factors account for the atmosphere of turmoil and indecision now surrounding the question of Nigerian local government. In the first place, organizational patterns are being reconsidered—an inevitable consequence of the change from four Regions to twelve States, and of the destruction of much of the local government apparatus in the war-torn sectors. Secondly, few observers of Nigeria's past would defend the local government system as it was operating during the mid and late 1960s. Especially in the former Western Region, local governments were underfinanced, poorly staffed, and wastefully competitive.

Conferences on local government, which began in 1969, are an indication that this decade may bring as thorough a reconsideration and reorganization in this area as in the nature of federal structures.[16] Specific matters to be settled will depend on basic decisions about the allocation of functions to local government. Informed Nigerians have learned the lesson from the world's recent economic development problems that development must originate "from below." The people must be motivated somehow toward participation in projects that improve their own local living standards. Effective local administrators who are familiar with local issues and deficiencies are more likely to cope

16 Institute of Administration, University of Ife, *The Future of Local Government in Nigeria*, Ile-Ife, Nigeria: University of Ife Press, 1969.

successfully than are officials in distant state capitals. Unfortunately, Nigerians have not to date achieved the right balance. As one UN advisor stated in 1969:

In the past local governments may have been given too many responsibilities in Nigeria and, in many instances, inadequate arrangements were made for the provision of staff and finance to enable them to discharge their extensive duties. During the last year or two the pendulum has swung and it is now evident that local governments, at least in some States, have been left with far too few responsibilities.[17]

A recent study of Lagos Government reached a similar conclusion; the combination of political instability and takeover of many functions by the federal government has dampened "the enthusiasm of regional or national governments for sharing powers within their domains."[18]

Finally, administrators may have to face another unsettling suggestion. The western concept of bureaucrats who administer without political favoritism is criticized as irrelevant by a growing number of Nigerians. The hoped-for "new politics" of Nigeria in the 1970s will not be the faction-ridden politics of the 1960s. The new mood will be dominated by a concentration on development tasks. As the political scientist Essien-Udom expressed it, in such circumstances, "politics is inseparable from administration." Civil servants, he clarifies, "should be committed to a development ideology."[19]

[17] L. Rowland, "The Relationship Between State and Local Governments," in *Ibid.*, p. 123.

[18] Babatunde A. Williams and A. H. Walsh, *Urban Government for Metropolitan Lagos*, New York: Praeger, 1968, p. 160.

[19] E. U. Essien-Udom, "The Responsibility of the Higher Civil Servants in Nigeria," in Adebayo Adedeji, ed., *Nigerian Administration and its Political Setting*, London: Hutchinson, Educational Ltd., 1968, pp. 128–129.

CHAPTER FIVE

Political Attitudes
and Nigerian Politics

IN THE NORTH, the "Twelve State Decree" of May 27, 1967, split an area unified 150 years previously by Uthman dan Fodio's holy war (see Figure 5). Overnight adjustment to the new situation, though certainly not likely, seems to have been eased by the influence of local emirs. Like leaders of the non-Moslem tribes of the middle belt, the Emirs of Zaria, Kano, and other Moslem centers are not unhappy with their new influence. The "monolithic" North appears to have been more fragile than most observers suspected; its unity was quite dependent, in fact, on the presence of a strong-willed sultan at Sokoto. The new sultan, however, does not seem inclined to attempt any reconstruction of Ahmadu Bello's power. In any case, this may no longer be possible, given the constitutional division of the North into six states, and the disappearance of the conditions that fed Ahmadu Bello's obsession with a united North. Infiltration of civil service and commerce by easterners is not likely to be rapid as long as they remember the pogroms of 1966.

Clearly, Northern Nigeria must now be studied in a new light. The longer the six state governments have to become entrenched and develop their own interests and momentum, the more remote the likelihood of recentralization. The principal changes in northern society resulting from the decree are (1) the long-sought autonomy of non-Moslem tribes such as Tiv, who will

Figure 5

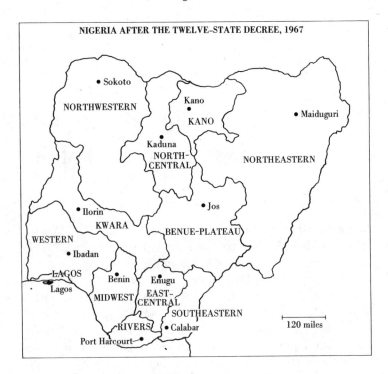

NIGERIA AFTER THE TWELVE-STATE DECREE, 1967

exert more influence than previously through their representation in the army and through their respective state governments, and (2) the destruction of the apparent Hausa-Fulani solidarity which controlled the First Republic.[1]

In Southern Nigeria, creation of new states in 1967 has had a different impact, as Table 5 indicates. In the South, the major tribes were less affected by direct division. Yorubaland remains virtually intact as Western State, while the Ibo heartland is more or less synonymous with East-Central State. Ironically, these situations present more difficulties than the more obvious carving

[1] Discussions of postcoup adjustment in northern Nigeria are found in Schwarz, *Nigeria*, ch. 9, and in Panter-Brick, ed., *Nigeria Politics and Military Rule.*

Table 5. Nigerian Demography after the Twelve State Decree
(based on November 1963 census)

State	Population	Area (in square miles)	Persons per square mile
Northwestern	5,733,297	65,143	88
North-Central	4,098,305	27,108	158
Kano	5,774,842	16,630	339
Northeastern	7,893,343	105,300	78
Benue-Plateau	4,009,408	38,929	95
Kwara	2,399,365	28,672	82
Lagos	1,443,568	1,381	251
Western	9,487,526	29,100	239
Midwestern	2,535,839	14,922	168
East-Central	7,227,559	11,310	711
Southeastern	3,622,591	11,166	263
Rivers	1,544,313	7,008	233
Total	55,770,056	356,669	156

SOURCE: *Nigeria Year Book: 1970*, Lagos: The Times Press, 1970, p. 21.

up of the North. Many Ibo, previously encouraged by scarcity of land and unemployment to leave Iboland for the Northern Region and for non-Ibo cities such as Lagos and Port Harcourt, have since 1967 returned to what became Biafra and then East-central State. Civil war and reconstruction have compounded the problems that led them to migrate in the first place.

In the Yoruba Western State, old internecine arguments have combined with difficult economic conditions, making the state hard to govern.[2] These problems of adjustment to the twelve state system and to reconstruction after the civil war provide a context for our treatment in detail of the diversities of Nigerian political attitudes. For our purposes, it is helpful to attempt some generalizations about the political attitudes of "Nigerians" in comparison to citizens in other types of political systems.

[2] For postcoup adjustment in the six southern states, see Schwarz, *Nigeria*, chs. 10 and 11; B. J. Dudley, "Western Nigeria and the Nigerian Crisis," in Panter-Brick, ed., *Nigerian Politics and Military Rule*, and K. Whiteman, "Enugu: The Psychology of Secession, 29 July 1966 to 30 May 1967," in Panter-Brick, ed.

Democracy and Nigerian Political Attitudes

In the early 1960s, Africanists became accustomed to citing Nigeria as an example of the successful transplanting of Western democracy. Professor David Apter's assessment was that in the confrontation between traditional, Western, and Marxist forms of organization and values, the Western transplantations would win out through a process of "institutional transfer" from the colonial power.[3] Another scholar's inference was that Nigeria would develop democratically because her leaders "have a contempt for demogogy."[4]

Are Nigerians collectively a "democratic" people compared to Frenchmen, Russians, or others? The President of Tanzania, Julius Nyerere, wrote just after his country became independent in 1961, that it was "absurd" to ask if democracy could survive in postcolonial Africa. In insisting that "democracy, in its true sense, is as familiar to the African as the tropical sun,"[5] Nyerere was assuming that the same attitudes conducive to successful "village democracy" in traditional African settings could serve the democrat in the new, bureaucratized African state. Nyerere's point served a polemical purpose, but social scientists generally believe that widespread changes must occur in individuals undergoing the transformation from traditional agrarian to modern industrial society. Furthermore, if this assumption is true, it would seem anachronistic for those same leaders who have repeatedly indicated their intention to revolutionize their peoples' economic situation and attitudes to imply that the political tendencies requisite for modern democratic life are already present.

Without losing sight of the important differences between Nigerian ethnic groups, we are able to make some contrasts on this large scale by referring to cross-national surveys of politically relevant attitudes in which Nigerians are one of several comparison

[3] Not specifically developed for Nigeria, David E. Apter's analysis can be found in Ghana in Transition, New York: Atheneum, 1963.

[4] John Hatch, Africa Today—and Tomorrow, New York: Praeger, 1962, p. 40.

[5] Julius K. Nyerere, "Democracy and the Party System," in Rupert Emerson and Martin Kilson, eds., The Political Awakening of Africa, Englewood Cliffs, N.J.: Prentice-Hall, 1965, p. 122.

groups. According to Alex Inkeles, whose team of interviewers collected data on political participation in six developing countries, the "syndrome" of modernity includes:

Freedom from traditional authority or, stated positively, identification with, and allegiance to leaders and organizations transcending the parochial and primordial; interest in public affairs validated by keeping informed and expressed through participation in civic action; and an orientation toward political and governmental processes which recognizes and accepts the necessity and desirability of a rational structure of rules and regulations.[6]

Inkeles discovered through interview data, that a layer of "participant citizens" who share these qualities exists in Nigeria, Argentina, Chile, East Pakistan, India, and Israel, and, therefore, that "the concepts which had been fashioned for the study of political orientation in more developed countries provide a meaningful basis for measurement of the political attitudes, values, and action of the common man in underdeveloped countries." [7] These are participant citizens on the national level in the new countries, not to be confused with members of traditional "village democracies," although as Chapter One indicated, some traditional political cultures can make a more painless adjustment to modern participant citizenship.

Understanding the difference between "mango-tree" (traditional) democracy and participant citizenship is essential for a grasp of politics in the new countries. Village organization is based on family units, rather than central authority. The traditional village's basic concerns have little to do with modern productive goals, and its typical product—a stable environment in which family units can survive—flourishes in conjunction with traditional values. Conversely, modern educational and industrial systems, which may not look very "democratic," are analogous settings to the modern developing country, with its "more definite collective goals" and "national purpose." [8]

[6] Alex Inkeles, "Participant Citizenship in Six Developing Countries," *American Political Science Review* 43, no. 4 (December, 1969): 1122–1123.
[7] *Ibid.*, p. 1127.
[8] *Ibid.*, p. 1140.

Examining the roots of participant citizenship shows how unlikely it is that Nigerians will be drawn deeply into the national system, with or without democratic leanings, unless those modern values are present. Inkeles's study shows the importance of formal education as a "school" for participant citizenship," but points more strongly than other works on political attitudes to factory experience as a second causal variable.[9] Such findings are obviously important for our assessment of Nigeria's potential for successful construction of mass participant citizenship.

Most empirical work has shown a positive relationship between standard of living and political participation indices.

> Good citizenship is . . . a kind of luxury which can be "afforded" only by those who have secured a standard of living above the minimum required for mere survival. Of course, active citizens are no luxury, but rather a necessity for running a modern polity and the society which relies on it.[10]

Even among African examples, Nigeria ranks with the "comparatively underdeveloped" countries, as Table 6 demonstrates. With low rates of literacy and industrialization, it is unlikely that Nigeria's politically relevant strata run very deep. Nigeria's underdevelopment would suggest a shallow basis for potential "activism"

Table 6. Socioeconomic Indices Compared
(range 1.00 to 0.00)

United States	1.00	Yugoslavia	0.19
West Germany	0.71	Philippines	0.17
Israel	0.67	Dominican Republic	0.16
Japan	0.60	Brazil	0.16
Poland	0.45	Egypt	0.14
Cuba	0.35	Nigeria	0.02
Panama	0.31	India	0.00

SOURCE: Hadley Cantril, *The Patterns of Human Concerns*, New Brunswick, N.J.: Rutgers University Press, 1965, p. 194.

[9] Compare, for example, Gabriel A. Almond and Sidney Verba, *The Civic Culture: Political Attitudes and Democracy in Five Nations*, Boston: Little, Brown, 1965.
[10] Inkeles, "Participant Citizenship," p. 1134.

at the national level. This does not imply that the few participant citizens are the only group with any potential for action, but it does mean that the percentage of the population equipped for continuing, cooperative political participation is limited. Furthermore, we have so far stressed only that socioeconomic development is necessary as the basis for "participant citizenship." Political activism, of course, may take either a positive or a negative form.

What, then, is the political role of the vast majority of people in a traditional, agrarian country like Nigeria? According to Inkeles,

To leave men in a condition of poverty so extreme that they are outside politics, in effect, non-citizens, is to create an apathetic mass which is not integrated in society and cannot be mobilized for the purposes of national growth and development.[11]

The fascinating thing about the recent history of the political role of the "apathetic masses" is its mercurial nature. During the late colonial era, nationalist political organizations were able to justly claim mass emotional support from their populations in the struggle against European colonialism. Post-World War II nationalist leaders were able to accomplish what the urban, professional, middle-class African elite of the interwar era had proven incapable of doing—communicating the evils of European rule in terms the masses could understand. The enemy was clearly definable and tribal differences were set aside. We shall see in our subsequent treatment of the development of Nigerian nationalist groups and political parties, that ethnic suspicions were submerged only briefly in favor of the common cause, and quickly resurfaced by the early 1950s.

The impact of these developments on the attitudes of Nigerians by 1962 can be inferred through interview data collected for *The Pattern of Human Concerns*, a twelve-nation study directed by the psychologist, Hadley Cantril. Compared to people in the eleven other countries, Nigerians mentioned political instability and national disunity frequently. In spite of the absence

11 *Ibid.*

of any real or perceived foreign threat, Nigerians in 1962–1963 ranked highest of the twelve national samples in fears for their country's future. The interviews revealed "the apprehension of Nigerians about the consequences of regional and tribal factional-ism that so stand in the way of the achievement of national unity." [12]

Other features of the 1963 Nigerian "public mind" were re-vealed in the Cantril study. Two years after independence, Ni-gerians certainly did not conform to Inkeles's subsequent view of apathetic masses. At that time, Nigerians were "sensitized," "involved and enthusiastic," and "bubbling with aspirations." Compared to "lethargic" Brazilians and Indians, who voiced few concerns and aspirations, Nigerians had high hopes for personal and national progress, but also seemed to sense the difficulties ahead. According to Cantril, "once a people are awakened, their very backwardness can serve as an incentive for their striving, if they sense the potentialities available to remedy their lot as appears to be the case, for example, among Nigerians. . . ." [13]

Certainly Nigerians were introduced, at least in vague terms, to the potential of the modern world by their leaders, whose promises extracted support for the independence movement, and for regional solidarity against other ethnic groups. By early 1963, there were some clear national "winnings" that appeared to vali-date the promises that had been made, but other aspects of the interview data show how fragile was this euphoria. When re-spondents were asked to rate the potential for themselves and their nations, a high percentage of "no response" reactions re-vealed the inability of Indians, Brazilians, and Nigerians to think in terms of concrete developments. Although more politically awakened than the other two groups, probably because of pride in their new-found independence, Nigerians were still only "waiting in the wings" of national politics.[14]

---

[12] Hadley Cantril, *The Pattern of Human Concerns*, New Brunswick, N.J.: Rutgers University Press, 1965, p. 175.
[13] *Ibid.*, p. 230. For greater detail see the Nigerian background study done as a preliminary to *Patterns of Human Concerns*: Lloyd A. Free, *The Attitudes, Hopes, and Fears of Nigerians*, pp. 26–27.
[14] *Ibid.*, p. 234.

After a decade of turmoil, interview data gathered in 1970 would probably have shown that Nigerians had lost many of the vague euphoric hopes of 1960–1962, as the fears they had indicated about ethnic hostilities and political instabilities have materialized. This was generally true of the politically relevant strata by the mid-1960s. Inkeles's survey team found that in Nigeria "those who score high on participant citizenship are more often anomic and hostile, and . . . dissatisfied with the government's performance as well." [15]

Must we assume, then, that democratic politics is impossible in Nigeria? Political scientists are by no means united on the question of how closely democracy is related to the level of economic and social development.[16] The fact that many industrially advanced or advancing states are not constitutional democracies has caused this confusion. Preindustrial societies are quite unlikely to be constitutional democracies, but it is hard to overlook agrarian Denmark, or the United States (pre-1840) as exceptions. Among new countries, the "guided democracies" usually depend on strong charismatic executives rather than on features of constitutional democracies, such as freedom to dissent and form legal opposition, free elections, mass communications, rule of law and restraints on the power of the executive, bureaucracy, police, and army. Even guided democracy has not been notably resilient. In Nigeria, such a system may be harder to replace with a generalized affiliation to a national leader than almost anywhere else. The independence struggle produced no single leader of the caliber of Nkrumah, Sukarno, Kenyatta, or Nasser, who could rise above tribal identity. Even Azikiwe has usually looked more "Ibo" than "Nigerian" to most members of other tribes. Finally, General

---

[15] Inkeles, "Participant Citizenship," p. 1129.
[16] For example, the development theory of Gabriel A. Almond and G. Bingham Powell, in *Comparative Politics: A Developmental Approach*, Boston: Little, Brown, 1966, indicates that modern political systems (those with structural differentiation and substructure autonomy), can be totalitarian or democratic. However, some theorists who stress socioeconomic development as a cause of political system changes posit an inevitable trend toward democracy: for example, Robert A. Dahl, *Modern Political Analysis*, 2d ed. Englewood Cliffs, N.J.: Prentice-Hall, 1970.

Gowon does not seem to be the sort who is interested in a personality cult.

Basic Nigerian political reactions have generally been ethnic, as the course of organizational politics surveyed in Chapters Six and Seven will demonstrate, and specific political attitudes also serve as examples of ethnicity. During the decade before independence, different ethnic styles led to deep misunderstandings between North and South and between Ibo and Yoruba. Aristocratic northern leaders, accustomed to obedience from their masses interpreted the booing by southern crowds as a serious social affront, not as a specific objection to hesitancy over the "self-government by 1956" call by southern leaders. Since independence, the political stakes are higher, and the ethnic rubric has served as a frame of reference for virtually every act. One Western political scientist observed in 1965, that although "on the whole, the original Constitution has been observed . . . all parties were careful to observe the law . . . [and] the struggle for power has been conducted within the framework provided, . . . the spirit has been violated a number of times."[17] The quest for power dominated the events of the First Republic, and that power was used to enhance the position of the tribal groupings with which the individual was allied. The quest for power in its own right is natural and defensible, as the Minister of Culture's attempt to lure the young teacher in Chinua Achebe's novel, A Man of the People, shows. "I want you to come to the capital and take up a strategic post in the civil service. We shouldn't leave everything to the highland tribes . . . our people must press for their fair share of the national cake."[18] According to one Nigerian official, Chief Balogun: "When it suits our purpose we quote conventions surrounding the British system. When it again suits our purpose, we close our eyes to certain practices, all in the name of Nigerian way of life." [19]

It is questionable whether this Nigerian power struggle, which

17 Mackintosh, "Nigerian Democracy," p. 614.
18 Achebe, A Man of the People, p. 11.
19 Mackintosh, "Nigerian Democracy," p. 618.

tends to overshadow the niceties of constitutional provisions, will be fundamentally altered by the new twelve-state structure. On the one hand, the scope for influence by individual politicians has been potentially increased: There are now thirteen cakes to be carved up instead of the previous five. On the other hand, the potential for personal wealth and power to destroy the system from the center, as it did the First Republic, is impossible to assess. We can only be sure we understand the foundations of Nigerian political attitudes: political influence is sought for sub-national (personal and ethnic) purposes, and events are interpreted in the ethnic context. It is always an "Ibo coup," an "anti-Yoruba trial," or an "antinorthern" decree.

Ethnic Division and the Effects of Political Socialization

As we have seen, most Nigerians react to political challenge within a context of ethnic assumptions. To understand Nigeria's political development, and the prospects for a stable future, we must examine the roots of these basic attitudes. An important question is whether Nigerians will be infused with a more national outlook than in the past. We must survey political socialization activities and agencies in Nigeria to find the causes of current attitudes, and determine whether there is a basis for the growth of a "national" political culture.

In the absence of evidence to the contrary, we must assume that political attitudes in Nigeria, as in all political settings, derive largely from experience in the family unit. Political scientists conclude that, by and large, "the family transmits politics to the children." [20] In Nigeria, as elsewhere, this implies that two types of political information derive from family life—specific political attitudes and latent reactions toward authority, cooperation, and other social values. Hence, in Nigeria, the easterners' achievement orientation no doubt stems in part from a stress on

[20] Herbert Hyman, *Political Socialization: A Study in the Psychology of Political Behavior*, New York: Free Press, 1959, p. 52.

competition, aggressiveness, and "hustle" in family and village life. Analyses of Ibo traditional culture have often noted their stress on individual initiative, material success, equality of opportunity, innovativeness, and marketplace orientation. Recent empirical research validates the anthropologists' view of the Ibo. "The stereotyped image of the modernistic, achievement-motivated, and aggressive Ibo came into vogue because it was to a great extent accurate."[21] Such attitudes were propagated by traditional styles of political socialization, predominant among these, the family. In Chinua Achebe's *Things Fall Apart*, Okonkwo frets because his son does not fit his conception of "manliness," and at age twelve "was already causing his father great anxiety for his incipient laziness."[22] A large proportion of northern Nigerian society shows a quite different value system from the prevailing secular culture of the eastern peoples. Social relationships were traditionally based on client–patron situations, which all had "inequality of status of the associated persons as a common characteristic." [23]

How important are the basic social values derived from family experience as determinants of political attitudes? The *Civic Culture* survey of five countries concluded that occupational and educational experiences were most important for molding attitudes toward participation than was socialization in the family,[24] but more recent research does not support this finding. An attempt to establish the relative impact of three main agents of political socialization—family, school, and workplace—by carefully controlling all intervening variables has restated the importance of the familial environment. With more precision than previously, Langton's comparison of political socialization in the United States and Caribbean countries indicates the central role of family

21 Audrey C. Smock and David R. Smock, "Ethnicity and Attitudes Toward Development in Eastern Nigeria," *The Journal of Developing Areas* 3 (July, 1969):509. The Smocks argue, however, that other southeastern tribes appear to be as oriented toward these values as do the Ibo. For example, p. 505.

22 Chinua Achebe, *Things Fall Apart*, New York: Fawcett Publications, 1964, p. 17.

23 M. G. Smith, *Government in Zazzau: 1800–1950*, p. 31.

24 Almond and Verba, *The Civic Culture*, ch. 10.

influence.[25] In the Nigerian environment, which has stressed tribal identity and unity as barriers against the Ibo (or Yoruba, or northern) "menace," overt, ethnic political socialization does little to encourage a cooperative, civic, national outlook. We now turn to latent and surface political socialization in the Nigerian educational system, which might have been a means of offsetting the subnational affiliations encouraged by the family and ethnic group.

POLITICAL SOCIALIZATION IN NIGERIAN SCHOOLS

During my seventh grade, I remember a course entitled "Pennsylvania Studies." To say that the course made more than a vague impression on me would be incorrect. Compared to the near-total immersion in national concerns, my education in state and local affairs was insignificant, if not trivial. Today's American social studies students are exposed to even more nationally oriented issues, aided by such publications as *Dateline Series, Junior Wall Street Journal*, and others.

Schools have always been vehicles of political socialization in the United States, but have had much less success than intended. In spite of the conscious effort to instill a sense of civic duty and patriotism in young Americans, there is little proof that "civics" leaves much impression. Perhaps because of the success of the American family and elementary school as national political socializers, and the resulting high redundancy of information at the secondary level, according to Langton's survey, there were no cases "in which civics training was significantly associated with the students' political orientations." Langton points to differences between the importance of various agents of political socialization in the new countries and in highly developed political systems. According to him, the political socialization potential of school systems in underdeveloped countries is probably higher than in the United States. "In societies at different stages of development from the United States . . . traditional norms often clash with the modern values promoted by the political elites.

---

[25] Kenneth P. Langton, *Political Socialization*, New York: Oxford University Press, 1969, p. 159.

Under these conditions where information redundancy is low, policy makers may lean heavily on the formal curriculum as an agent of change." [26] One might suspect that political elite who desire drastic, rapid change would attempt to separate children from their tradition-oriented families in order to more completely immerse them in the new values. The political education roles of the Chinese commune system and of Khrushchev's boarding schools were to serve as such an agent of change through directed political socialization.

The Nigerian educational system has never had the opportunity to serve as a truly national agent for creating political attitudes. British control instituted an educational pattern similar to Britain's. There was little direct civics training, but much stress on "character-building." Perhaps this was just as well, judging from the products of French colonial education, also patterned after the mother country's system, which is high in overt citizenship training. Colonial powers were hardly likely to see value in a mass political consciousness which would make colonies even harder to govern. Naturally, colonial Africans discovered that "history" meant the history of Britain and her Empire, not of Nigeria, and that the heroes were Wellington and Lloyd George. A typical holiday was King George V's birthday, and English became the language of educated people. [27]

In his landmark study of political socialization, Charles Merriam listed eight factors contributing to civic education: schools, government agencies and officials, patriotic organizations, political parties, mass media, political symbols, languages and literature, and love of locality. [28] Half these items obviously overlap, lying neatly within the formal educational system. In a traditional society—new state, where the institutions controlled by the state are involved in "countersocializing" people away from old loyalties, the schools are well situated to spread acceptance of national

---

[26] Ibid., p. 177.

[27] On Nigerian's educational system and political socialization, see Ayo Ogunsheye, "Nigeria," in James S. Coleman, ed., Education and Political Development, Princeton, N.J.: Princeton University Press, 1965.

[28] Charles E. Merriam, The Making of Citizens, Chicago: University of Chicago Press, 1931.

political symbols, national culture, and loyalty to the new country as an institution. Under the Nigerian colonial constitutional system that became increasingly federalized after 1939, "in no sphere of governmental activity was the principle of diversity pursued to the same extent . . . as in education." [29] Only at the university level was there much federal government responsibility for budget, and at lower levels virtually all educational functions and agencies were controlled and financed by the regional governments.

Educational decentralization also hindered the development of a Nigerian political culture by widening the gap between the North and South in terms of progress. Islam's disinterest in modernizing northern education, in contrast to Christian missionary zeal in southern schools, created an "educational gap" that spurred the South's more rapid development.

Finally, decentralization contributed to the non-Nigerian nature of education in the colony. There were some sporadic attempts to bring Nigeria-related content into the curriculum, beginning with the Teachers' History and Geography Handbook for grades one through four in 1933. However, several specific factors hindered the growth of a Nigerian focus in educational content. Secondary education certificates were earned by passing examinations tied to a British curriculum, and textbooks were produced by English commercial publishers. Perhaps most important, Nigeria's universities, which developed after World War II, "are not Nigerian universities; they are British and American universities where Nigerians can take good degrees having international currency without knowing anything about Nigeria." [30] This remark by a British analyst of Nigerian education in the mid-1960s, shows Nigeria's inability to produce teachers who could inculcate students with values relevant to the new nation's problems even after several years of independence. It is no wonder that one Nigerian educational planner wrote in 1962: "Nigerians and their leaders do not as yet look up to the schools

---

[29] Arikpo, Development of Modern Nigeria, p. 104.
[30] L. J. Lewis, Society, Schools and Progress in Nigeria, London: Pergamon Press, 1965, p. 101.

as instruments for the conscious fostering of a Nigerian consciousness or solidarity." [31]

This situation is changing, but slowly indeed. After the brief, abortive attempt at centralization under Ironsi in 1966, Nigerian constitutional provisions now continue to give the twelve states control over education exactly as the four regions previously had. The new realities are likely to produce change in the North, where states do not coincide with one solid Hausa-Fulani cultural block. Attention will also be focused on the schools in East Central State, where teachers will be unlikely to get away with glorifying "Biafra." The fact remains, however, that education is still "regionalized," and appears likely to remain that way.

One source of possible impetus for an increasingly Nigerian approach to educational content might be from the universities. In fact, fundamental change has occurred there. In the past decade, research by Nigerian and Western social scientists has attempted to reinterpret Nigeria's past and present achievements and problems. Research centers at Ife and Ibadan are compiling and analyzing materials from Nigerian art and literature. Studies of Nigerian history are modifying the Eurocentric views of Nigeria's past found in most published works, which have treated Africa as the passive "Dark Continent" dehumanized by Europe's slave trade, "rehumanized" by European missionary-explorers, and finally "civilized and brought to freedom" by European colonial regimes. There are healthy signs of intellectual maturity in carrying out the task. According to the director of the University of Ife's Institute of African Studies, Dr. S. Biobaku:

This enterprise is beset with pitfalls. It has its own dangers. First it involves a rediscovery of the true past of Africa and the Africans, but this must not be romanticized unduly; it must not degenerate into chasing a past glory that never existed. There must be no pandering to the African jingoists by simply rejecting one extreme view of regarding Africa as having no worthwhile culture whatsoever and embracing the other, of idealizing everything African. Secondly, the magnitude of the task of reorientation should not be underrated. It must be remembered that the unfolding of a culture which has long been in decay is

[31] Ogunsheye, "Nigeria," in Coleman, ed., *Education and Political Development*, p. 134.

more than a lifetime assignment for any scholar. It can be accomplished only after prolonged study and research involving several generations of scholars. Thirdly, there is the danger of falsifying findings in order to conform with ephemeral notions of past glories or to suit some transient political necessity. On no account should the scholar compromise his academic integrity or connive at the enthronement of mediocrity just because it pleases.[32]

The tedious nature of this process is compounded by the many steps in transferring the new materials to school curricula. Research scholars must inform teachers, and manuals for lower levels must be made available. Finally, ethics inherited from colonial education, which stand in the way of adoptive attitudes necessary for this process, must be changed. "Many of the expatriate staff and some of the Nigerian intellectuals are reluctant to recognize that Nigerian culture and organization of society are worth studying by undergraduates."[33]

Mass Media as Sources of Political Attitude Formation

Among the small percentage who have become involved in the wage sector of the economy, occupational viewpoints and experience in organized groups modifies traditional socialization by family, village, and tribe. Those Nigerians who found employment in the civil service, police, and military went through a similar process. Finally, the independence struggle itself served to infuse in many Nigerians a new sense of activism and political competence, which had been lacking among colonial subjects generally. These group experiences are dealt with in subsequent chapters, but their importance as political socialization agents can be summarized. Perhaps unintentionally, members of these groups were instructed in the ways of modern organization, a development that spurred the secularization of Nigerian political culture. It is important to recognize, though, that comparatively few Nigerians were involved in such modern aspects of life.

[32] Lewis, *Society, Schools, and Progress in Nigeria*, p. 116.
[33] *Ibid.*, p. 113.

This discussion has questioned whether Nigerian political socialization is up to the task of molding a national political culture. Many American students will regard suggested reforms of the random socialization patterns at work in Nigeria as Machiavellian social engineering. We tend to accept, even glorify, our seemingly unplanned systems of political socialization, while ignoring the cement at the base of that system; underlying unities, such as our views of the "model American," and the "American way of life." We must remember that these underlying unities have yet to be created in Nigeria.

POLITICAL COMMUNICATIONS

If we were asked to explain the features of American life that contribute to the underlying consensus in our society, we would no doubt include our impressive array of intercommunications. Americans are not only physically mobile, we also live within a vast web of instantaneous communication and mutual contact, now dominated by television. Countries like Nigeria face the task of molding a similar type of identity among their citizens, but ironically, lack many of the prerequisites which make our communications system something we take for granted. Since nine-tenths of all Nigerians are illiterate, political communications would be proportionately more enhanced by use of radio and television than in more developed countries. But Nigeria finds telecommunications difficult and expensive.

In the past, Nigeria's outspoken press partially offset the colony's economic backwardness, adding a surprising amount of vibrancy and excitement to colonial politics, and playing an important role in political socialization as well. Since its beginnings in 1859, the British held a libertarian view of the press in Nigeria, allowing vigorous, sometimes strident, criticism of colonial policies by nationalists like MacCauley and Azikiwe. In an age when the notion of libertarian "freedom of the press" is seriously questioned even in its "homeland," Britain and America, the lack of restrictions on Nigerian journalism until the mid-1960s was quite remarkable. Because the situation has changed so much during the last decade, it is hard to classify Nigeria's mass media system today. For example, Nigerian mass communications are not typical of any of the four theoretical types cited by Siebert and his associates, who assume that mass communications in a political system "always take on the form and coloration of the social and political structures within which it operates. Especially, it reflects the system of social control whereby the relations of individuals and institutions are adjusted." [34]

In pure form, none of these basic theoretical options, categorized in Table 7, are appropriate for Nigeria. While the degree of governmental control of mass media may seem necessary to the leaders of a new country, the media are likely to be foreign-owned and perhaps ideologically incompatible with the leadership's intentions. New research on the role of media in modernization continues to emphasize the importance of linking mass media content to personal, face-to-face opinion leadership. To produce this coordination, a measure of governmental control is necessary. However, the political communications in a mobilization polity must be reciprocal, keeping leadership informed about the reactions of people to governmental policy and programs so that governmental action retains relevance. Some of the potential for critcism in a "free press" must be maintained. A brief survey of political communications structures in Nigeria illustrates some of these dilemmas.

THE PRESS

While Nigeria's press has long been renowned for its independence and vigor, it has frequently demonstrated an irresponsibility which a new country can ill afford. Most newspapers concerned themselves with personal and tribal accusations and supports during the First Republic, rather than with treatment of national issues. Since then, foreign affairs have been generally neglected. These situations are rather easy to explain. Nigeria's

[34] Fred S. Siebert Theodore Patterson, and Wilbur Schramm, *Four Theories of the Press*, Urbana, Ill.: University of Illinois Press, 1963, pp. 1–2.

Table 7. Types of Mass Media Organization

	Authoritarian	Soviet-Totalitarian
Origin	England, Sixteenth and Seventeenth Century Current examples: France 1958–1969; most "new countries"	U.S.S.R, and partially in Nazi Germany, Fascist Italy Current examples: U.S.S.R; Chinese Peoples Republic
Reason for Development	Philosophy of "absolute monarchy"	Marxist-Leninist-Stalinist thought
Purpose	Support government in power; help carry out government policy	Support government— party dictatorship; mobilize society for actions
Who Has Access to Use of Media?	Recipient of royal patent	Members of govern-ment—party elite
Means of Control	Patents, license by guilds	Constant surveillance of media operators by higher elite levels
Degree of Censorship	Occasional	Constant
Content of Censored Material	Criticism of govern-ment and officials	Criticism of party objectives
Type of Ownership	Mixed public and private	Public

SOURCE: Adapted from F. S. Siebert, T. Patterson, and W. Schramm, *Four Theories of the Press*, Urbana, Ill.: University of Illinois Press, 1963, p. 7.

largely privately owned press traditionally fit the "libertarian" mold: The people cared little for foreign news, and therefore received little. Politics was in fact ethnic and personal and was reported as such.

Libertarian	Social Responsibility
England after 1688 Current examples: has ceased to exist in pure form	U.S. and England in twentieth century. Current examples: most countries which previously used libertarian form
Writings of rationalists and natural rights thinkers	Theories of U.S. "Commission on Freedom of Press." Lord Reith of BBC
To entertain; to provide independent check on government	To uplift standards of both entertainment and public service functions (e.g., criticism of government)
Anyone who can afford to, or can "make news"	Anyone who has "something to say"
Depends on assumption that free exchange of ideas leads to truth Court litigation	Community opinions; action; professional ethics
Occasional	Occasional
Defamation; obscenity; indecency; "treason"	Invasions of private rights and interests of society
Private	Mixed

After 1964, the journalists' independent role was steadily reduced. Attrition began with a hotly debated Press Law, defended by governmental spokesmen on the grounds that newspapers were rumor-mongering and disrupting the faith of Nigerians in democratic government. Some disputed this view, arguing that there was a decreasing amount of democratic government to be defended. According to a Nigerian journalist studying at Wisconsin:

> The act was passed against stiff opposition by the press and the general public during the festering period of the NPC/NNDP coalition that plunged Nigeria into chaos shortly afterwards. It was at a time when the press, led by the Daily Express and the Sunday Express, was exposing some of the shoddy activities of the ministers; and when the politicians . . . were fighting back to maintain the status quo at all costs.[35]

The law provided for a fine or a 1-year jail term for anyone "who authorizes for publication, publishes, reproduces, or circulates for sale in a newspaper any statement, rumour or report, knowing or having reason to believe that such statement, rumour or report is false."[36] Further, the defendant would have to prove that before publishing the report concerned "he took reasonable measures to verify the accuracy of such statement, rumour or report."[37] In November 1965, the Amalgamated Press papers were closed after one of their editors was prosecuted under the provisions of this act.

Since 1966, the military regime has stated a belief in the virtue of Nigeria's free press traditions. Gowon had this to say to the officials of the Daily and Sunday Times about the role of the press during the crisis period in 1966–1967.

> I cannot tell them what to do since we do not dictate policy to any press here; they have been independent as they ought to be. The press has to tell the truth, to be objective and honest so that the people can rely on what they print. They should tell us off when they feel we are wrong and commend when they feel it is worth while: we can take it.[38]

The dangers of a controlled press situation are obvious. Any scrutiny of government actions is avoided; "unpleasant" events,

---

[35] David Dmazo Edeani, review of T. O. Elias, Nigerian Press Law, in Africa Report (December, 1970):41.

[36] Schwarz, Nigeria, 126–127.

[37] Rosalynde Ainslie, The Press in Africa: Communications Past and Present, New York: Walker, 1966, p. 222.

[38] Quoted by T. O. Elias, Nigerian Press Law, London: Evans, 1969, p. 129.

such as strikes, ethnic hostilities, and clashes go unmentioned under the Press Law. The readers will learn of these events anyway, so all that is gained is a lessening of the media's credibility. Meanwhile, a "brain drain" of the news media occurs as first-rate journalists depart; the *Daily Times* of Lagos has lost Peter Enahoro, who perceptively lampooned Nigerian politics as "Peter Pan." In spite of its stated views, the military government has not reversed the deterioration of press freedom. In reply to the Federal Commissioner of Information and Labor's view that today's Nigerian journalists lack the stature of their progenitors, the journalism student quoted above answers, "The problem with the Nigerian press is not simply that it lacks a corps of competent practitioners, but that it has been forced into dangerous docility by too many restrictive laws." Countertrends in the Nigerian press include the growth of government papers such as the *Daily Post*, the *Sunday Post*, and *Sketch*, and the development of a government news agency. In defense of these trends, an American scholar has concluded:

The pattern of government controlled papers is being firmly established—and may in time, as some predict, be the only form of press ownership. Although the old maxim about government papers always being dull seems to apply as much to Africa as elsewhere, they are undoubtedly providing news and information of a sort generally unavailable before. They tell the government's story—explain policies, publicize leaders, and thus contribute to the much-needed realization of "nationhood" and in general espouse national purposes. Certainly an authoritarian press has an important role to play, especially if it concerns itself with news and information of significance to its readers and makes more of an effort than the press has done to date to reach and provide reading matter for the newly literate in the small towns and villages. . . . There is a real need to develop an infrastructure of small regional papers supplying local news. . . .[39]

RADIO AND TELEVISION

The history of Nigerian telecommunications has differed substantially from that of the press, but it is likely that the eventual

[39] William A. Hachten, "Newspapers in Africa: Change or Decay?" *Africa Report* (December, 1970):25–28.

result will be similar. The Nigerian Broadcasting Corporation (radio) is a statutory corporation owned and operated by the government, though a small number of commercial stations do exist in competition with NBC. One factor not familiar to American students, but significant in the political communications profile of many new countries, is the pervasiveness of foreign radio broadcasting. Nigerians are quite likely to be using their shortwave bands (Americans seldom do) which will allow them access to Voice of America, Radio Moscow, Radio Peking, the British Broadcasting Corporation, and other foreign networks. Therefore, the Nigerian Broadcasting Corporation faces severe competition for its audience. In an illiterate country, this and other features of radio broadcasting are quite significant. Radio can be used as a modernization tool or a means of political control. The high priority given to radio broadcasting facilities by planners of coups d'état indicates its potential in the latter category and the concentration of radio facilities in the new countries has been one factor which facilitated the rash of coups we have recently witnessed. As with airports and strategic ground traffic control points, one radio station is easier to capture than many.[40]

In content orientation, NBC still reflects its inheritance from the principles that dominate radio broadcasting in Britain. The BBC has been guided since 1927 by a succession of civil servants who have prided themselves on being nonpartisan and free from government control. Much of their "improve and educate the public" ethic rubbed off on NBC. Since neither national radio service depends on advertising for revenues, each can well afford to eschew the pure entertainment function of American television. Though the ownership structures differ, perhaps the best American analogy to Nigerian telecommunications is our Public Broadcasting Corporation (National Educational Television). Presently, however, a new purpose is asserting itself on Nigerian radio: national mobilization and development. It remains to be established whether this use of radio differs from the old BBC

[40] Edward Luttwak, Coup d'Etat: A Practical Handbook, New York: Fawcett, 1968.

approach. "I should not for a moment admit that a man who wanted to speak in favor of racial intolerance had the same rights as a man who wanted to condemn it." [41] This view of the present Director-General of BBC (indicating that while BBC may be politically nonpartisan, it is morally partisan) would not differ from the current perceived task of the Nigerian Broadcasting Corporation.

Though Nigeria is one of the few African countries with television networks, the importance of this medium (expensive to the consumer and therefore not widespread) lies in the future, as part of the plan of mobilization for development. It will be further discussed in Chapter Eight.

To conclude, news media in Nigeria are moving toward the authoritarian model. Existing media are increasingly under pressure to temper criticisms, act "constructively," and promote development policies. To further the cause of modernization, there is also a noticeable increase in government pamphleteering. Certain state governments are supplying the bulk of this effort, exhorting the citizenry to engage in suggested self-help projects, pay taxes, etc., but as yet not all seem equally aware of the potential of this form of propaganda. Rivers and Northwestern State Governments are more active pamphleteers than the others, with Rivers especially prolific in documents welcoming the visits of officials of other states. These welcoming statements are used to promote development-oriented messages Rivers State wants to convey to its people.

[41] Sampson, *The Anatomy of Britain Today*, pp. 649–650.

CHAPTER SIX

Pressure Groups

ONE CAN FIND organizations expressing political attitudes in Nigeria that are similar to those operating in stable democratic systems. The observer can classify them as: (1) associations created specifically to bargain and exert pressure in favor of political goals, for example, trade unions; (2) institutions intended for some nonpolitical purpose, for example, the army or bureaucracy; and (3) basic groupings of a social, religious, or tribal nature, which predated the modern political dialogue. All have been active during Nigeria's political development, and therefore constitute "pressure groups." Apart from these categories, there are spontaneous, relatively unorganized groups, such as found in American politics, that also express political aims.

There are some important differences between the styles of group politics in "developing" countries and in industrialized states. One of the most prominent features of advanced, representative democratic systems is the profusion of autonomous political demands, stemming from a welter of specific occupations and outlooks. The thousands of political interest groups and their lobbyists at work in France, Britain, or the United States dominate the process of presenting political interests. American political parties have generally been successful in boiling down these demands into two major (though sometimes blurred) alternatives. France's political party system has usually been less successful at this task.

As our analysis of current society demonstrated, the bulk of the Nigerian public is preindustrial and rural, though "politically relevant" because universal suffrage has been attained. This fact tends to simplify the study of political pressure groups and also to make less significant in Nigeria some of those groups which are very crucial to the political process in Britain or France, such as labor unions or small businessmen's lobbies. One might expect that as economic development, detribalization, and social change proceed, Nigerian politics will be progressively more influenced by groups of this kind.

Conversely, among Nigerian organizations that have consistently expressed basic political interests are several that are formally restrained in Western democracies, notably the army and government bureaucracy, whose primary functions supposedly lie outside the political arena. There are two main consequences of this situation: (1) Either the small governing elite decides to mobilize the people by taking over their present organizations and linking them to the governing structure; or (2) In more representational systems, the groups compete, ordinarily to the advantage of the governmental bureaucracy's and other central institutions' political demands.

Neotraditional Groups

As Nigeria progressed toward self-determination with democratic structures, a deep sense of kinship to one's ethnic group underscored a person's feelings toward the new political issues. The impact of a legislature with increasing power was seen in terms of what the change would mean for Ibo, Tiv, or Hausa. Soon after constitutional changes began to indicate increased participation for Nigerians, traditional ethnic units responded through organizations that could survey the progress of constitutional change and protect the interests of that tribe.

Associations designed to promote traditional ethnic groupings arose soon after the new element of British rule was established. As early as 1918, the Egba Society, representing the Egba section of Yoruba, emerged to sponsor Egba Yoruba in Lagos and Egba-land. Egba Yoruba realized that decision-making power had been taken away from their king, the Alake of Abeokuta. Many Egba decided to put their trust in a flexible organization that could intervene with the new sources of power: the government in Lagos, commercial interests, and the new Nigerian elite. Other factions among the Yoruba quite logically founded similar societies. Contacts between Yoruba subgroups demonstrated the importance of pan-Yoruba identity. In the late 1930s and the war years, Yoruba promotional activity was directed at acquiring overseas scholarships for Yoruba students and obtaining jobs for fellow tribesmen. Cultural identity led Yoruba students in London to create the Egbe Omu Oduduwa (Society of the Descendants of Oduduwa, the legendary father of the Yoruba).

Yoruba political focus was stimulated by the threat posed from east of the Niger. The populous but poorer Ibo and their eastern neighbors facing similar problems emigrated in increasing numbers in all directions as the colonial power imposed peace throughout the area. Prizing Western education and competition between each other on individual and village levels, the Ibo quickly saw an advantage in organized cooperation. Ibo who were already located outside their homeland were most conscious of the efforts that would be required for Ibo progress. The Ibo Union, formed in Lagos in 1933, was founded by a British-trained physician concerned about the advancement of his people. The Union's history shows the neotraditional nature of the typical "tribal association." Willing to use modern tactics in a modern political setting, and led by a partly Westernized elite, the Ibo Union's basic identity was unmistakably ethnic. Ibos outside Iboland were organized into these unions during the 1930s, and in 1943 an Ibo Federal Union was created to coordinate tribal fund raising activities and policies.

As politics intensified after 1945, these traditionally based associations carried on their mutual rivalries, leading to a vicious press war in 1948. When political parties were created by the more activist leaders, the Ibo Federal Union and Egbe Omu Oduduwa were allied to the party that emerged in each region. An ethnic flavor to party politics was unavoidable.

The northern equivalent to these neotraditional associations reflected the more controlled nature of northern society. The Ibo, Yoruba, and other southern ethnic associations developed as federations of local "tribal improvement" clubs, which had grown more or less spontaneously. The North witnessed a relatively short period of such efforts before cultural and ethnic associations were superceded by *Jam'iyyar Mutanen Arewa*, or Northern Peoples Congress (NPC), a hastily arranged organization controlled by the emirates. NPC was quickly transformed into a political party. Northern awakening was stimulated by the obvious and growing threats of Ibo expansion and Yoruba cohesion at a time when increasing political access was necessary for all who would compete successfully within the increasingly democratic political context.

Ibo Union, Egbe, and Jam'iyyar were the most significant neotraditional associations because they derived from the three major ethnic groups, and because they had close ties with the three main political parties. However, there were many other illustrative examples of ethnically based associations designed to ease the transition from village to town life. The *esusu*, or contribution-savings-credit clubs of Ibo located in western cities, and similar *adashi* among urban Hausa with regular cash incomes, had more limited functions. Other associations were more multifunctional, providing a locus for social, athletic, religious, political, and financial activity.[1] The Afikpo Town Welfare Association among the Ibo in the Eastern Region operated in several realms in addition to serving as a stimulus for improvements.[2] Enugwu-Ukwu Patriotic Union was founded "to serve the interests of its members, and to seek the welfare of our town." The Union arranged meetings every 2 years to promote unity among the Enugwu citizens who had left the village; lobbied for an improved market facility and post office site; and mobilized successful

[1] On multifunctional urban organizations, see Kenneth Little, *West African Urbanization: A Study of Voluntary Associations in Social Change*, London: Cambridge University Press, 1966.

[2] Thomas Hodgkin, *Nationalism in Colonial Africa*, New York: New York University Press, 1956, p. 86.

resistance to the warrant chief system of indirect rule, which was abolished in 1944.[3]

These tribally based associations were not "traditional" in the sense of predating European contact. They developed after the colonial era began and their function was to aid in the adjustment of the tribe to social change in the colony. They operated from an ethnic, traditional basis to provide new security for those uprooted from traditional patterns of life. They eased the path for Nigerians entering a strange, new social setting and preserved an African flavor in the ideas and organizations that emerged to protest British domination. Further, neotraditional organizations helped to educate the new Nigerian leadership. Perhaps most important of all, they provided a communications network which prevented particularly the urban Nigerians from becoming an isolated, inarticulate mass. From a negative standpoint, neotraditional associations contributed to the distinctly regional flavor of nationalism during the 1940s and 1950s.

Posttraditional Voluntary Associations

Some interest group functions were performed by a host of clubs, leagues, unions, and associations that arose, again mostly in urban settings, but differed in that they were "detribalized." Many such sport clubs, teachers' clubs (formed by graduates of one school such as Lagos' Island Club), and women's unions, were based not on tribal identity, but on the diversity of city life. However, we should not overstress the "modernity" of most voluntary associations in Nigeria or any new country by imagining that they were completely divorced from old ways. We have only to think of traditionalism (ethnic, racial, and parochial) as found in American politics. According to Gabriel Almond:

> The West is more like the non-West than we sometimes think. Even in the most differentiated and specialized political systems in the West, such interest groups as families, status groups, and religious

[3] Dilim Okafor-Omali, A Nigerian Villager in Two Worlds, London: Faber, 1965, p. 140 and chs. 14 and 15.

communities affect the political process. And in most of the non-Western countries—however "underdeveloped"—the beginnings of functionally specialized political parties, and associational interest groups such as trade unions and trade associations, may be found.[4]

Trade Unions

Nigeria is a preindustrial society with only 5 to 10 percent of the population in wage-earning roles; it is not surprising, therefore, that the trade unions have not been continuously influential pressure groups. Before World War II, a few workers' organizations existed for civil servants, railway workers, and teachers, but most workers were unskilled illiterates, unorganized and unorganizable. Before the Trade Unions Ordinance of 1938 legalized labor organizations in Nigeria, as the British Parliament had done for British labor activity in 1871, Nigerian unions were not allowed to organize any type of concerted action for bargaining purposes. Colonial governmental practice was to classify many services as "essential" which meant that "emergency powers" could be invoked. Administratively, colonial labor departments kept close watch over accounts and activities of unions, and discouraged political affiliation. The result of this policy "was to give labour departments a real or potential power rare in Britain's own industrial experience." [5] In more politically unified African settings, the colonial arrangement gave way to a merger of government, party, and unions. This trend has restricted the union's autonomy in collective bargaining, although political influence by top labor leadership is sometimes enhanced.

In Nigeria's absence of political unity, government-union relationships after independence continued much as before. Nevertheless, students of politics in the new countries have come to expect much from organized labor as a political interest group because there are so few other organized interests, and because

---

[4] Gabriel A. Almond, "A Comparative Study of Interest Groups and the Political Process," in Harry Eckstein and David E. Apter, eds., *Comparative Politics: A Reader*, New York: Free Press, 1963, p. 407.

[5] Ioan Davies, *African Trade Unions*, Baltimore: Penguin, 1966, p. 42.

trade unions have usually learned organization skills and tactics from European mentors. However, Nigerian trade unions have not been as significant as in most other African cases. In Nigeria, few close relationships between trade unions and nationalist political movements developed before independence, and there have been only isolated cases of successful political pressure on postindependence government. The Nigerian Trades Union Congress, a "peak" organization which claimed an affiliation of 80-odd member unions, was associated with NCNC from the 1944 origin of Azikiwe's party until 1950. However, TUC contributions (to NCNC) in money and other types of support were negligible during that time. The high point of the labor-nationalist alliance during the colonial period was 1949, after the shooting by police of twenty miners in Enugu, Eastern Region.

Labor leaders were generally more radical than the southern Nigerian political leadership, and only when the politicians' demands fit closely with the grievances of Nigerian labor, on such issues as work conditions and foreign control of economy, was there much cooperation. After the National Emergency Committee, formed to deal with the Enugu grievances, had fallen apart, labor leaders drifted toward a more radical perception of Nigerian problems. Only in the Northern Region was there lasting affiliation between unions and the major party: NPC and the Northern Mineworkers' Union were organizationally allied, but the relationship was distinctly NPC-controlled.[6]

Usually, the political activities of Nigerian labor have been outside the mainstream of politics. The labor leader Nduka Eze was one of the organizers of the "Zikist" movement which sponsored demonstrations, street actions, and disruptive tactics, of which Azikiwe and the NCNC themselves did not approve. After the Zikists were broken up in 1950, labor leaders reasserted their political ambitions periodically by creating labor parties, but they have never achieved much significance.

Except for some of the northern cases where the unions had

6 Elliot J. Berg and Jeffrey Butler, "Trade Unions," in James S. Coleman and Carl G. Rosberg, Jr., *Political Parties and National Integration in Tropical Africa*, Berkeley: University of California Press, 1964, pp. 342–345.

little autonomy within the NPC-directed politics, political leaders tended to distrust the laborites, not without some cause. Furthermore, in the North, the structure of the NPC as a regional alliance of traditional elite devalued the participation of organized labor. Finally, another drawback to pressure group effectiveness by workers was their failure to organize on an industry-wide basis. Much of the dissension among Nigeria's unions has derived from international division among workers. After World War II, a World Federation of Trade Unions (WFTU) was formed by leaders from most countries with significant labor movements. By the late 1940s, with the crystallization of the cold war, western unions walked out of WFTU, leaving that organization in Communist hands, and formed the International Confederation of Free Trade Unions (ICFTU).[7] Table 8 shows the competition between these two organizations, which has combined with personal and ethnic rivalries within Nigeria to encourage division in labor organizations.

There are other reasons for Nigeria's history of politically weak organized labor. In France's colonies, centralized labor federations were encouraged, while Britain preferred to allow "locals." Furthermore, because a high proportion of jobs have been in the government sector, control over potentially disruptive union activity has been deemed more necessary, and has been easier to assert. Students should keep in mind that government workers in America are discouraged from attempting to exert the types of union pressures that are employed against our railways, or against such companies as General Motors Corporation. In Nigeria, a higher proportion of activities are government-related or administered.

In spite of the roadblocks facing organized labor in Nigeria, there have been three significant periods of labor unrest, demonstrating "conclusively that the Nigerian labor movement had come of age and was capable of united and effective action."[8]

[7] One of the best accounts of the impact of international labor dissension of African unions is Davies, *African Trade Unions.*

[8] Robert Melson and Howard Wolpe, "Modernization and the Politics of Communalism: A Theoretical Perspective," *American Political Science Review* 45, no. 4 (December, 1970):1125.

Table 8. Dissensions in Nigerian Labor

	World Federation of Trade Unions (WFTU 1945, Communist dominated after 1948)	Attempts to Unify Workers	International Confederation of Free Trade Unions (ICFTU, non-Communist since 1948)
1942		Nigerian Trade Union Congress (NTUC) General Strike	
1945			
1954–1957	All Nigerian Trade Union Federation		
1959	Trades Union Congress of Nigeria		National Council of Trade Unions of Nigeria Nigerian Trade Union Congress
1961	Independent United Labor Congress		United Labor Congress of Nigeria
9/1963 to 1/1965		Joint Action Committee (JAC) General Strike	
12/1970		United Committee of Central Labor Organizations (UCCLO)	

After the first two of these occasions, 1945 and 1964, labor solidarity soon gave way to the more customary ethnic political patterns, but these cases do provide evidence for theories about the resilience of traditional institutions. As one argument had put it "too frequently, political development has been seen in terms of a struggle between 'nationalism' and 'traditionalism,' the fall of the latter thereby signalling the rise of the former."[9] In 1964, labor leaders were supremely successful in organizing a national strike, but when they attempted to mold labor solidarity into support for a national "labor party," workers withdrew their allegiance.

When it came to questions of the pocketbook—to questions of salary and conditions of service—Nigerian workers held much in common irrespective of their diverse communal attachments. . . . But when it came to the election of parliamentary candidates in 1964, their communal identities were "triggered" once again. . . . The moment the strike was concluded, the lines of political cleavage within the nation were redrawn, socio-economic identities once again being subordinated to the communal identities of region and nationality.[10]

A third period of labor solidarity has dominated the post-Civil War years. The leadership of trade unions has not lost the ability to mobilize support for specific economic objectives. UCCLO, led by Michael Imoudou, was formed in October 1970, under conditions similar to those in 1964. As formerly, a commission was appointed to study wage levels, but the workers were still unhappy about the sluggishness of government response to their demands. Price controls were attempted with little sucesss, and by mid-1970 inflation was a serious concern. Workers also attempted to commit the government to rescinding the antistrike decree, initiated in 1969. A serious labor crisis is undoubtedly brewing in the 1970s, but not until that crisis has been met will we be in a position to judge the increasingly popular hypothesis of political scientists: Effective "national labor" can coexist with neotraditional communal organizations. The test will be whether UCCLO will continue to coordinate an organization of national

[9] *Ibid.*, p. 1126.
[10] L. Schätzl, "The Past and Future Role of Coal in the Energy Market of Nigeria," *Nigerian Journal of Economic and Social Studies* XI, no. 2 (July, 1969):115–141.

scope, or whether, like JAC in 1964, UCCLO will step aside, allowing ethnic attitudes to resurface.

Political pressure groups will obviously be greatly affected by the military government's choice of domestic priorities for the early 1970s. Labor relations and power resources policies show this political connection well. During this decade Nigeria's transportation, power, and heavy industry will have to adjust to the advent of hydroelectricity and petroleum as the major power sources. Electricity from Kainji Dam on the Niger, and the switch by Nigerian Railways to diesel fuel, mean that new markets must be found for the country's large deposits of low-grade soft coal. One political advantage of the proposed iron and steel complex would be the continued employment of several thousand coal miners. The Enugu miners, a political force since pre-World War II times, would resent failure to reopen their mines while the Okapa mines (opened when the civil war interrupted operations at Enugu) are expanded. Thus, development policy, reconstruction, and political interests overlap.[11]

Political Interests of the Professionals

No survey of pressure groups in western democracies can ignore the influence of organized professionals, especially doctors and lawyers. In America we are accustomed to an abnormally high frequency of lawyers in government and politics, and because of their strategic location within every community and their collected financial power, we expect to hear from their spokesman on any issue that concerns them. Their position in Nigeria is more difficult for us to understand. As members of the small, less traditionally minded elite, Nigerian professionals are heavily concentrated in the cities, while the masses are in rural areas. Their potential for mass persuasion is further reduced by the huge educational gulf between themselves and their popular audience. In a national propaganda campaign, their organization might not have

---

[11] Melson and Wolpe, "Modernization . . .", p. 1127.

nearly the same impact, for example, as the American Medical Association's 1949 campaign against Truman's medical care proposals. However, during the First Republic, doctors and lawyers both used methods of political influence quite related to their sources of strength. While American doctors concentrated on convincing large numbers of people to turn their legislators against government involvement in medical insurance, Nigeria's doctors went to work directly on the legislators themselves. In 1963, the Nigerian Medical Association squashed the Lagos Health Services Bill, which would have set up eleven health centers for free treatment in Nigeria's capital city. The political influence of doctors, as well as professors, lawyers, and other professionals, is enhanced by their scarcity. With only 2 doctors per 100,000 people in Nigeria, each doctor's value to society is great compared to France, Britain, the United States or the U.S.S.R., where the figures per 100,000 are 86, 42, 181, and 133 respectively. These are bargaining points Nigeria's medical personnel could use when a new politico-medical issue arises.

Selected events would indicate that lawyers and other intelligentsia shared an inordinate degree of political influence during Nigeria's First Republic. A concerted attack by lawyers, the intelligentsia, and the press defeated the Preventive Detention Act in 1963, causing one observer to comment: "It is significant that the only serious opposition the Government has encountered in the Federal House of Representatives has been when it tampered with the Press, the lawyers, and the doctors."[12] For that political scientist, these were "favorable signs" in an era of concentrated power by Nigerian politicians.

As the country's prosperity increases, professional and commercial groups are becoming stronger and they are eager to insulate themselves from politics. In doing so, they build up their own legal and financial defenses and become small centers of power capable of offering some resistance to political pressure.[13]

Generalizing about the influence of groups is a hazardous procedure, however, and tends to show as much about the as-

[12] Mackintosh, "Nigerian Democracy," p. 626.
[13] *Ibid.*

sumptions of the analyst as it does about the groups. A second political scientist, observing Nigerian politics during 1963, when the Republican Constitution, the Preventive Detention Act, and other pivotal issues were under consideration, concluded on the basis of his interviews of various political elite that

Intellectuals and professionals, as such, seem to be as much under the sway of the wielders of political control as any other group. . . . Lawyers as such, and as a group, have little influence potential. The Nigerian Bar Association, for instance, appears to be paralyzed on controversial issues because of the divergent interests of its membership, a good proportion of whom are beholden to the regional government and to political parties through positions as legal advisors.[14]

In conclusion, most occupationally distinct elite groups of professional and intellectual status have reaped great socioeconomic rewards, but seem to wield political power only on those rare occasions that bind them together for a common cause. Usually their relationship to politics is similar to that of the workers: subordination to the organizations that represent communal ethnic units. There are postwar indications, especially among teachers who have defied that antistrike decree (North-Central State Strike of early 1971) that Nigerian occupational groups are as capable as those anywhere of perceiving demands and courses of action, but there is little concrete proof that communal (tribal) attachments have disappeared for good.

The new Nigerian federal structure may exacerbate divisions within professional groups to the extent that it allows intermingling (competition) between the communities. The effective National Union of Teachers, founded in 1931, was significant on a national level only on specific economic issues which cemented teachers in the very different school systems of South and North.[15] Separation into two systems may have actually aided in what little cooperation there was. It is hard to imagine what the response

[14] Henry L. Bretton, "Political Influence in Southern Nigeria," in Herbert J. Spiro, ed., Africa: The Primacy of Politics, New York: Random House, 1966, p. 74.

[15] David B. Abernethy, "Nigeria," in David G. Scanlon, ed., Church, State and Education in Africa, New York: Teachers College Press, 1966, pp. 211 ff.

of Nigerian professionals will be to the existence of twelve local power centers.

Women

The vantage points offered Nigerian women for the exercise of political power and influence have varied immensely. Ibo women traditionally enjoyed "a high socioeconomic and legal status." [16] Ties between Ibo women, either in Iboland or in the growing Nigerian cities, were strengthened by the system of exogamous kinship, which linked women of Ibo villages. No woman could marry a man in her village, and since new married couples traditionally settled in the husband's village there were always women "on the move" between villages. Though descent and succession were patrilineal, matrilineage was important in legal and emotional terms, and women were vigorous participants in village life.[17]

In northern Nigeria, on the other hand, traditional Moslem values limited women's role in public affairs. They were ineligible for succession to noble titles, were secluded residentially, and were legally treated as minors until married.[18] More recently, women were denied recourse to political action as the franchise developed during the past two decades. Yoruba women, in spite of the significant intrusion of Islam into the Western Region have reacted to and benefitted from modern political development more in the style of the Ibo. In Yoruba towns, much of the market activity is carried out by women, who have been well organized to preserve their own interests. The Egba (Yoruba) Women's Union of Abeokuta conducted literacy classes, operated maternity and child-health services, and a weaving cooperative, and was in the forefront of the 1948 agitations resulting in the resignation of the Alake of Abeokuta.[19] Among Ibo women, as one might

[16] Uchendu, *The Igbo of Southeast Nigeria*, p. 87.
[17] M. M. Green, *Ibo Village Affairs*, part III.
[18] M. G. Smith, "Introduction," in Mary Smith, *Government in Zazzau: 1800–1950*, and pp. 225 ff.
[19] Hodgkin, *Nationalism in Colonial Africa*, p. 90.

expect, traditions of political activity are well established. The Aba Riots, or "women's war" of 1929 stemmed from rumors that a planned census would result in special taxing of the women, especially the growing number of market women.[20] Fifty women were killed before order was restored, but these illiterate women had shown their ability to organize quickly and cooperate for a political goal.

Their dominance of the commerce of the southern Nigerian cities places women in an unquestionable position of potential influence. The Lagos Census of 1950 showed 84 percent of the city's small businesses owned and run by women.[21] Actual political influence derived from their strategic location is questionable. Professor Bretton's interviews of commercially influential women in 1963 led him to conclude that, though "market women" organizations were a crucial part of the political communications network, their political power was marginal.

Data collected indicate that whatever influence potential may be attributed to these leaders is largely confined to matters related to trading, construction of market stalls, market fees, trading facilities and contracts, retail distribution, and the like. In exchange for recognition of at least the most pressing of their economic demands, leaders of this group, and most of the women generally, seem prepared to accept blindly the leadership of the party, loyally and even fiercely giving it their wholly uncritical support on all other issues, including women's rights and questions of integrity and honesty in public office, as well as questions related to the survival of democratic institutions.[22]

Agriculture-Based Groups

Most Nigerians are rural people, and it is crucial to determine what types of basic political interest avenues and organizations are available to them. As a rule, such organized expression is found only in connection with the cash crop sector.

---

[20] Ottenberg, in Bascom and Herskovitz, *Continuity and Change in African Cultures*, ch. 11.
[21] Little, *West African Urbanization*, p. 124 and ch. 7.
[22] Bretton, in Spiro, ed., *Africa: The Primary of Politics*, p. 61.

One of the first political actions organized by Nigerian agricultural groups was the 1937 resistance to cocoa price fixing by European-owned firms. Most of this effort was promoted by the Nigerian middlemen rather than by cocoa growers themselves. In most cases, efforts to improve conditions in agriculture have come, not from ground-level organizations but from above. Agricultural credit banks are examples of investment structures in which the farmers who are supposed to benefit have suffered from political opportunism. However, in spite of the failures of agricultural organizations, Nigerian farmers have been and are politically significant.

The most recent examples of political activity by farmers offer more evidence of the important role of political associations. Western State cocoa farmers have been angered throughout the 1960s by increased taxes and lower prices for their crops. An organization called "Agbeparoo" was formed to organize protest among disgruntled Yoruba. Tafa Adeoye, a cocoa growers' leader, has helped to mobilize farmer dissidence especially since a poor crop in 1968 compounded the farmers' economic woes. Furthermore, a recovery in world cocoa prices during the late 1960s was not passed on to the farmers, who were, however, taxed to share the financial burdens of civil war.

Agbeparoo tactics are significant in their own right. The cocoa farmers drew support and sympathy from Awolowo against the former Western State Governor, Brigadier Adebayo. Though the rioters have earned concrete gains in the form of increased cocoa prices paid in 1969 and 1970, their specific winnings were achieved as part of the larger aspect of intra-Yoruba tension. The cocoa farmers remember the years concluding the colonial era, which preceded the 1962 Western Region crisis as years of prosperity. Prices were high and the Action Group looked out for their interests.[23] Then, in rapid succession, Awolowo was ousted from political power, and tried for treason. Akintola took office with northern help, at a time when cocoa prices fell drastically. The world market suggested a price drop before 1965, but the region's

[23] Schwarz, Nigeria, pp. 275–276.

Marketing Board supported the farmers' prices, and with the fall in price from $300 to $168 per ton in 1965, hatred of Akintola's regime intensified. The coup in 1966, recounted in Chapter Three, may in part have been triggered by the Western Region's agricultural troubles.

The Political Role of Government Institutions

One of the conclusions to emerge from this account of organized political interests in Nigeria is that groups from which we expect considerable political influence in Western countries (labor, professionals, farmers, etc.) have far less direct influence in Nigerian politics. Those groups tend to reflect the ethnic divisions that fractionate the society, and the politicians seem inclined to view them as bases of communal support rather than as independent power groups with concrete demands. This is true as well among the academic elite, the last group in which one would look for exclusivist ethnic affiliations. As soon as the important issue of staffing is at stake, ethnic loyalties take ascendancy. Disputes at universities at Lagos, Zaria, Nsukka, and Ibadan, indicate a surprising amount of pluralism among the academic community.[24]

The real powers behind Nigerian politics since independence have been (1) the top political party leaders before 1966; (2) the military leaders since 1966; and (3) the bureaucracy throughout the decade. Several general statements may be made regarding the exercise of political power by these groups.

The party elites can be viewed as a series of pressure groups because of the groundrules for Nigerian politics established during the First Republic. This is perhaps just as true of the "new class," in communist countries or the American and British leaders educated at the Ivy League's "Big Three" and at "Oxbridge." In a structurally democratic system, Nigerian politicians saw their constituencies in terms similar in one respect to the approach of the Soviet elite. Although the goals differed, Nigerian

[24] Ibid., pp. 46–50.

politicians followed their own desires rather than systematically assessing the demands and needs of their supporters.

The military leadership's political influence since 1966 is obvious, and can be partly understood through the discussion of governmental organization in Chapter Four. The influence of an army that has successfully carried out a coup d'etat is enormous, especially in comparison with its limited role in Western countries, which try to follow the civilian dominated model and restrict the military's political potential. The Nigerian army has decided such important political issues as war and peace; nonetheless, its leaders view their mission as a custodial one. In setting a timetable for construction of a new system of government and in enforcing stability until that new system is established, the army's interests are perceived as identical to those of the people.

The military also seeks its own goals, and it is instructive to identify how much these considerations influence their actions. During colonial times, Africanization of the officers corps and improved pay and working conditions dominated the army's political outlook. Political action was severely restricted by the dominant British civil-military ethic. One would expect that exservicemen, particularly those who served during World War II, would have been more politically activist than the military bureaucracy itself. However, once they were discharged and free from the direct control of British officers, their grievances were compounded enormously by severance from military life. No program of veteran resettlement was carried out by the colonial government, and "many of them were no longer interested in returning to their homes in the villages because there was nothing to attract them there. They had acquired new wants, new tastes and new desires which could not be satisfied in the villages."[25] Nigeria's exservicemen were unquestionably "ready to join the struggle against the colonial administration that had treated them so shabbily."

This was the case in most countries which became independent after World War II, having made some contribution to that war as colonies. As individuals, exservicemen were possibly no less

[25] G. O. Olusanya, "Ex-servicemen in Nigerian Politics," *The Journal of Modern African Studies* 6, no. 2 (August, 1968):226.

significant in Nigeria than elsewhere. As "General China" (one of Kenya's Mau Mau leaders) put it:

> I took back with me lasting memories. Among the shells and bullets there had been no pride, no air of superiority from our European comrades-in-arms. We drank the same tea, used the same water and lavatories, and shared the same jokes. There were no racial insults, no references to "niggers," "baboons" and so on. The white heat of battle had blistered all that away and left only our common humanity and our common fate, either death or survival. . . . I had learnt much, too, about military organization. . . .[26]

Political scientists have tended to stress the organized political role of de-activated soldiers in Africa's colonies, but in Nigeria's case this emphasis is unwarranted. The reasons for the political ineffectiveness of Nigerian exservicemen as a group are quite similar to the factors that have weakened labor, the professions, and the military. Even the Supreme Council of Exservicemen, formed in 1948 by a leadership which was quite aware of the dangers of noncoordination, proved ineffective because exsoldiers' primary loyalties belonged to a proliferation of local groups. Among the reasons cited for this "multiplicity of organizations" was "tribal politics, a dominant feature of the country's political life at that period."[27] The divisions within the nationalist movement encouraged exservicemen to suspect fellow exsoldiers from different tribes or regions. As with the groups considered above, exservicemen as an associational pressure group were weak internally in comparison to the organization of the political party to which its leaders gave allegiance. Ethnic divisions of the party system have weakened the basis of group organization.

> The greatest factor . . . making for the political impotence of the ex-soldier was that the nationalist movement, which should have given them the necessary encouragement and leadership, as in Ghana, was badly divided and lacking in courage.[28]

Another reason for expecting exservicemen's associations to

---

[26] Waruhiu Itote (General China), Mau Mau General, Nairobi: East African Publishing House, 1967, p. 27.

[27] Olusanya, "Ex-servicemen in Nigerian Politics," p. 229.

[28] Ibid., p. 231.

show an inordinate amount of "nationalist" reaction to politics is the assumption that the army is an ideal "melting pot," in which Ibo, Yoruba, etc., all wear the same uniform and where ethnic differences fade away. However, modernization does not progress totally at the expense of traditionalism. As our Vietnam experience has shown, mere participation in a modern organization may intensify traditional ethnic conflict while modernizing other thought patterns. The Nigerian armed forces as an institution are subject to these same processes, and any analysis of the political demands of Nigeria's military establishment must take this into account. If the civil war was largely the product of distrust between Ibo and non-Ibo officers, the military has obviously not functioned effectively as a modernizing agent in reducing tribal tensions.

As Chapter Four indicated, the army had clearly perceptible strengths and weaknesses when it became directly involved in Nigeria's politics. It was small, composed in January 1966 of 518 officers and 10,500 men. In the light of coups by far smaller armies in neighboring West African countries, this force was obviously adequate, especially considering that confidence in the political leadership was badly undermined and that no groups of comparable strength existed. But the army was badly divided along ethnic lines; most officers of the rank of major or above were Ibo, but most troops were from the middle belt minority tribes of Northern Region. The younger officers, lieutenants and captains, have made attempts since independence to redress the tribal balance, but those predominantly northern and western officers can expect a far slower rate of advancement. Rapid Africanization had provided the vacancies which officers had already occupied, and had made their superiors colonels at young ages, but by the middle 1960s, lower officer ranks felt stifled. They were understandably restive, and the slaughter of their Ibo superior officers in July 1966 reflects the depths of their disillusionment. Like the January "majors coup," the July "lieutenants coup" was based on rank and, therefore to some extent, on tribe.[29]

---

[29] For a discussion of the Army's organizational and ethnic texture, see A. R. Luckham, "The Nigerian Military: Disintegration of Integration?" in Panter-Brick, ed., *Nigerian Politics and Military Rule*.

With the rapid promotions of noneastern junior officers following the July coup, the federal army has become more internally cohesive. Neither Yoruba nor Hausa-Fulani elements are dominant at any level, and all of the 36 officers holding a rank of lieutenant-colonel or higher in January 1966 were easterners who joined the secessionist forces. The Nigerian army's political effectiveness prior to 1967 was obviously hampered by the confluence of tribal differences with "generation gap" anxieties. As Luckham has argued, the ethnic and regional identities alone are not sufficient to account for the violence of 1966.

They did not have the strength of compulsiveness in and of themselves to stimulate overt expressions of antagonism within the military in the face of the well-enforced and internalized fraternal norms of the officer corps. One can only adequately account for the sudden florescence of animosity in 1966 by viewing this as a contextual effect of instability and strain on tribal and Regional ties which then become outlets for the expression of a whole range of tensions both within the military organization and outside of it in the wider political context.[30]

Since the civil war's end, the political potential of Nigeria's military has been reduced by a far different factor. With federal forces exceeding 200,000 men after 3 years of war, the government faced the difficult task of demobilizing this large force.

Compounding this problem was the lack of discipline in evidence during the war itself. Federal units began to operate disruptively after Biafra's surrender. Wounded troops mutinied to enforce their demands for pay, and cases of uniformed lawlessness broke out in 1970. The tactics of such ad hoc groups are understandable under the circumstances, and certainly show the internal weakness of the military—a force strong enough to exclude politicians, but too weak to do much more. Finally, the excesses of some officers show that military government will have difficulty promoting the self-sacrificing ethics which guided Major Nzeogwu and other coup organizers in January 1966. There are still many officers, such as Gowon himself, whose values are shaped by their view of what their country and her people need, but others have obviously begun to eat their share of the "national

---

[30] *Ibid.*, p. 76.

cake." Years of civil war have schooled both groups in the tactics necessary to achieve their ends.

While the army's national organization might have been expected to provide the cement that would hold Nigeria together during the country's darkest hour, the police's role provided contradictory examples. A decentralized organization, the Nigeria police had become, by 1966, a tool for political control by each regional political party. Police ranks were more infiltrated by corruption, and reflected a far less unified or nationalized social composition. Ironically, the "primordialism" that erupted in 1966 had far less effect on the police than on the army, and while army ethnic factionalism was literally tearing Nigeria apart, the police were responsible for keeping the peace, such as it was.[31] While the army had become a menace to security, at times during 1966 the disciplined police force prevented Nigeria from completely falling apart.

As a political interest group, the police are likely to wield more national influence now that a clear power center can be identified, and political pressures do not divide them at subnational levels. The police have recently successfully resisted a campaign to disarm the on-duty officers, and have countered that attempt by advocating the use of automatic submachine guns to counter rising armed crime.[32] This step was taken in mid-1971.

Finally, the civil service must be mentioned as a politically significant institutional group. As in the case of the army and police, political ethics inherited from Britain (and shared by Americans) do not conceive of this group as a legitimate political force. We become annoyed when a Patrolman's Benevolent Association lobbies for its interests, or when the Pentagon "sells" new appropriations. Similarly, we expect, and no doubt obtain to a remarkable degree, nonpartisan service from civil servants of all types.

[31] For an analysis based on this hypothesis, see A. R. Luckham, *The Nigerian Military: A Case Study in Institutional Breakdown*, unpublished doctoral dissertation, University of Chicago, 1969, pp. 306–308.

[32] T. N. Tamuno, *The Police in Modern Nigeria*, Ibadan: The University Press, 1971. Tamuno calls for a centralized national police force. In view of the army's experience, it must be asked whether this would be a wise policy.

In less developed countries there are several conditions which render this ideal far less workable. As one political scientist remarked about five case studies of administrative problems in Western Nigeria: "How irrelevant seems the dichotomy, so dear to the Western constitutionalist, between 'politics' and 'administration', in contemporary Nigeria!" [33] One of the major reasons for this situation is the relative importance of Nigeria's civil servants. In a Nigerian government ministry, the commissioner since 1966 has ordinarily been a civil servant. Even before 1966, only the top person in each ministry was a politician; directly below him the professional civil service began, with the Permanent Secretary. This contrasts sharply with the United States, where there are several levels of politically appointed under-secretaries and senior assistant-secretaries. The obvious result is that Nigeria's top level civil servants filled decision-making positions of greater political significance than their American counterparts, even before military rule catapulted them to heights ordinarily occupied by politicians.[34]

Under military rule, Nigeria's bureaucrats feel less political pressure from below, and are more in position to pursue their own ambitions. In Ibadan, for example, a central slaughterhouse sought by various meat marketing interests since 1948 is now not likely to materialize until political party competition returns to Western State. Civil servants, who will have to sort out the contestants and submit to the strongest, do not look forward with glee to that day.[35] In a sense, Nigerian civil servants have more leisure to sort out their own aims while political party activity is temporarily suspended. Pressure groups that would besiege them with demands still exist, but only as fractionated, localized organizations, since groups require the leverage of a political party to carry much weight.

[33] F. M. G. Willson, "Foreword," in David John Murray, The Work of Administration in Nigeria, London: Hutchinson, 1969, p. viii.

[34] Joseph F. Maloney, "The Responsibilities of the Nigerian Senior Civil Servant in Policy Formulation," in Adebayo Adedeji, ed., Nigerian Administration and its Political Setting, London: Hutchinson, 1968, pp. 118–126.

[35] David John Murray, "Interest Groups and Administration in Nigeria," in Ibid., esp. pp. 39–42.

The bureaucracy's temporary commanding position is reduced by an internal difficulty. Nigerians seem less able than the British to manage smoothly the generalist-specialist setup of civil service instituted by the British. This concept, which was established in practice in 1954, draws on the British tendency to champion the talents of the well-rounded administrator while suspecting the limitations of the "narrow specialist." Nigerians have not resolved the dilemma of whether this bureaucratic model is appropriate in a situation where the informal communications network and "old school ties" that support it are not as developed, or not even perceived as socially desirable. Until this split is resolved, the Nigerian civil service will lack the cohesion required for identifying and promoting political options.[36]

To conclude, interest groups in Nigeria are generally weakly organized and incapable of continued political effectiveness throughout the national system. Even the comparatively strong institutions, such as the army, police, and civil service, depend more on the presence of a power vacuum than on their own organizational virtues. Associations, created specifically to achieve concrete gains through political activity, suffer from the vastness of the country, inadequate leadership and funds, and insufficient communications. Yet even they are occasionally situated to derive advantages from the power vacuum through strikes or other disruptive tactics. On balance, the institutions, particularly those connected with essential governmental functions, have the inside track. The British colonialists may have attempted to establish a nonpolitical ethic for these institutions, but the dominance of the army and civil service over Nigerian politics since 1966 is proof of their failure.

[36] These questions are debated in remarks by Adedeji and T. M. Aluko in *Ibid*.

CHAPTER SEVEN

Political Parties

By "DEMOCRATIC POLITICAL PARTIES" we usually mean organizations which employ their machinery for competing within a representative system for the support of voters. Between 1923 and 1966, Nigeria's representative machinery witnessed the development of many organizations that would qualify as "democratic political parties," serving the function of amalgamating political interests for interjection into the decision-making machinery. Differences between these political parties in terms of their size, durability, tactics, and cross-sectional representation were considerable. To trace the development of Nigeria's political parties we must take into account the growth of opportunities for representation as the franchise spread, and the reactions of the parties to this challenge. Finally, we will combine the pre-1966 political party experience with adaptations that have occurred in political patterns since then to draw some conclusions on what can be expected when, and if, politics formally resumes during the 1970s.

During the interwar period, early Nigerian political parties reflected the narrow representation of Nigerians on the Legislative Council. They were no more than small groups of followers surrounding influential persons. The Nigerian National Democratic Party (NNDP), founded in 1923 by the Nigerian engineer Herbert Macauley, was never a "mass party." There was no reason at the time to involve the masses, and the small Nigerian urban elite of lawyers and other professionals dominated the process of introducing Nigerian opinions and reactions into the LEGCO. Their aims appeared "nationalistic" because African freedom was advocated. But in practice, specific gains, such as creation of African universities and African representation in LEGCO dominated everyday political ambitions. Furthermore, NNDP's activities were limited for the most part to Lagos.[1]

Perhaps because of the success of some NNDP aims, the educational pace for Nigerians increased so that by the mid-1930s, a growing number of young Nigerians had reached a vantage point from which they could see more clearly the evils of colonial rule. Nnamdi Azikiwe and other members of this new elite were dissatisfied, and their impatience was exacerbated by the economic ills of the depression and the inadequacies of the NNDP in battling them. A radical Nigerian press, led by Azikiwe's *West African Pilot*, vigorously condemned the colonial and domestic enemies of this rising young elite. The Nigerian Youth Movement (NYM) with 10,000 members in 1938, took a more militant nationalist stand on most issues.

During the 1930s and World War II, Nigerian politics, still Lagos-centered, was a competition between NNDP (representing established professionals and traditional leaders who were able to rally votes from the largely Moslem Yoruba masses of Lagos) and the NYM (which was as much a political party as NNDP and derived support from the educated, Christian, urban elite, as well as from a partially detribalized working class of Yoruba and Ibo). NYM captured the LEGCO seats in 1938, but in 1941 Azikiwe broke with NYM, and in 1944 was convinced by a new youth group, the National Union of Students (NUS), to create a united nationalist front for promotion of constitutional change. Nearly all extant associations, unions, political parties, and youth groups accepted affiliation with the new front, called the National Council of Nigeria and the Cameroons (NCNC).

During this period of development in political party structures and leadership, the Nigerian countryside played little active part.

---

[1] On early political parties in Nigeria, see Richard Sklar, *Nigerian Political Parties*, Princeton: Princeton University Press, 1963, and Coleman, *Nigeria: Background to Nationalism.*

Lagos and London were the centers of the Nigerian elite, and mass support was not necessary or desired. Most westernized Nigerians looked down on the huge tribal masses as traditionalistic, backward people of little value in the struggle to modify British control.

World War II seemed to change this situation. The Nigerian elite saw the likelihood of a faster pace of constitutional change toward independence, since the war against fascism was also a war against "empire" as the birthright of Europeans. Britain could hardly fight such a war in good conscience without disclaiming a permanent empire for herself. The development of the United Nations, the texts of wartime agreements among the allies, and the obvious weakening of the colonizers (Britain and France) were factors which encouraged Nigerian nationalists.

The NCNC's creation reflected these developments, and the changed tactics of Nigerian leaders became obvious as soon as a specific issue emerged. Governor Richards's heavy-handed "announcement" of the new constitution allowed the nationalists to focus Nigerian attention on the tactics of the colonial government, although deemphasizing the fact that the new constitution was a considerable advance in the very direction the nationalists desired. NCNC arranged a national tour for Macauley and Azikiwe, rallying supporters throughout the colony. For this short period, tribal antagonisms were secondary to mutual disgust over British methods and reluctance to grant constitutional change. Even in the north, many urban and educated elements supported NCNC's positions, though the traditional emirs who held power by virtue of indirect rule were naturally hostile.

During the early postwar years, NCNC developed in a pattern similarly to that of the "fronts" or "congresses" in other African colonies. In some of these cases (Ghana, Tanganyika) the nationalist movement proceeded to lead toward independence populations who were more united by the common enemy of imperialism than they were divided by the traditional animosities, but the NCNC claimed in Rousseau-like fashion to represent the will of all Nigerians. For a brief period this appeared to be at least superficially true, but there was the important qualification that not many Nigerians were yet ready to be represented. However, in the short space of 4 years, the political party system was to change drastically, so that by 1950 it had come to reflect the deeper antagonisms and divisions within Nigeria.

A major reason for these realignments was that the colonial administration began to take the lead in the process of constitutional change. With the colonial enemy less apparent after 1949, Nigerians found themselves arguing over the specific provisions of the proposed revised constitution. Also, since London had in 1947 rebuked the NCNC leaders for their attempt to modify the Richards Constitution, internal arguments over tactics destroyed much of their common purpose, providing radicals within NCNC with an occasion to demand more drastic actions, such as strikes and boycotts. The result was the formation of the "Zikist movement," which was disowned by NCNC.[2]

The death of 21 miners in the Enugu coalmine strikes of 1949 caused a last rapproachment among Nigerian nationalists; but a National Emergency Committee formed to present the miners' case used the issue to promote self-government and soon fell apart. Discussions to prepare the MacPherson Constitution of 1951 involved leading Nigerian politicians in the procedural issues of a democratic system, to which Britain was obviously committed. The new constitution provided for three regional legislatures whose elected membership would appoint delegates to the Federal Legislature. Political party attention naturally focused on the elections that would provide regional legislatures, and the political party system began to change rapidly.

While the NCNC retained a nationalist orientation in preparing for the 1951 elections, Azikiwe's political enemies went about rallying Yoruba support. Though Azikiwe was an Ibo, his political power center was Lagos. When the federal capital was included in the Western Region under the new constitution, Azikiwe's opponents were offered a perfect chance to accomplish the task of rallying Yoruba chiefs and their people against the menace of

[2] The "Zikists" are described in G. O. Olusanya, "The Zikist Movement, 1946–1950," *Journal of Modern African Studies* 4, no. 3 (November, 1966):323–335.

Ibo control. Spearheading the Yoruba mobilization was a group of younger elite within the Egbe, who called themselves the Action Group (AG), led by the lawyer Owolowo. NCNC won the Lagos seats; but AG, by dominating most of the Western Region, formed the first representative government there, with Azikiwe the leader of the opposition.

NCNC was forced to transform itself from a national movement into a political party with an ethnic core, while AG underwent a change in the opposite direction: An ethnic association, the Egbe, became an election-oriented political party the AG, happy to have whatever non-Yoruba votes it could recruit.[3]

The slower rate of political party development in the Northern Region was caused by several factors: (1) education, industrialization, and urbanization levels were inferior to those in the Southern Region; (2) traditional leadership was strongly in control; and (3) the northerners did not participate as elected members in the LEGCO. Perhaps most significant was the interlocking and overlapping nature of the traditional system with the political ideas of the new elite. Graduates of Kaduna College were also sons of the emirs, and of Hausa-Fulani royalty in general. Attacks on British rule necessarily discredited the native administration system of the Moslem leadership, and were not countenanced. However, some small discussion groups did exist after World War II. These dealt at first with specific grievances of civil servants or teachers, and were becoming more politically minded by 1948.

More radical northerners, mostly lower level clerks, founded the Northern Elements Progressive Association (NEPA) in 1947 and were in contact with NCNC, with which they shared many aims. Several of the more moderate groups merged in late 1948 to form Northern Peoples Congress (NPC), which advocated political reform but had as yet no position of influence. NPC was more closely attached than NEPA to the administrative-social-religious power structure of the Northern Region and had as one of its aims the prevention of "southern domination." By 1950,

---

[3] The Action Group's development is recounted in Awo: The Autobiography of Chief Obafemi Awolowo, London: Cambridge University Press, 1960, ch. 14.

with northerners now suddenly aware of the implications of the impending regional elections, the differences between the two groups surfaced. The NEPA leaders transformed their scope of operations directly to the political arena, under the title of Northern Elements Progressive Union (NEPU) boldly declaring the evils of feudalistic northern administration. Internal social reform was NEPU's foremost avocation, and NCNC support its main sustenance. During the 1950s, effort by radicals to publicize NPC failed, thus clarifying the distinction between the two organizations, and NPC moderates countered by purging radicals from the group. When NEPU won the primary elections in Northern Region during 1951, NPC leaders quickly became aware of the consequences of tardy political action. They rapidly transformed NPC into a political party which overcame NEPU's lead and controlled the first Northern Region Assembly after the 1951 elections.[4]

Cementing the Regional Party System

As the political parties came to reflect basic ethnic divisions, AG and NPC chose to remain tribally based; and NCNC had little option but to secure at least those (Ibo) votes that could be counted on under the circumstances. During 1951–1954, the three groups of leaders concentrated on controlling their regional legislatures. Under the MacPherson Constitution, the central legislature was recruited "indirectly" from the regional legislators rather than directly from popular election. Politicians had begun to recognize that they only needed to secure the support of the federal-level delegates for their respective regional governments.

The 1954 Constitution, which regionalized many governmental functions and divided up the civil service accordingly, encouraged the political parties to focus on the regions, but NCNC leaders were anxious not to succumb to this regionalization process. How-

[4] A full account of NPC's growth is found in B. J. Dudley, "The Northern People's Congress," in Mackintosh, ed., *Nigerian Government*, pp. 358–405.

Table 9. Nigerian Federal Elections

Region	1954 Seats[a]	1959 Percent of total vote in region	
Western			
NCNC	23	NCNC	40.2
AG	18	AG	49.5
other	1	NPC	1.7
		other	8.6
Eastern			
NCNC	32	NCNC-NEPU	64.6
AG	3	AG	23.1
other	7	other	12.3
Northern			
NPC	79	NPC	61.2
Allies of NPC	5	Allies of NPC	
AG	1	AG	17.2
Independents and other	5	NCNC-NEPU	16.1
Lagos			
NCNC	1	NCNC-NEPU	55.9
AG	1	AG	43.8
		NPC	0.2
Southern Cameroon			
Cameroon National Congress	5		
Total			
NPC	79	NPC	28.2
NCNC	56	NCNC-NEPU	36.1
AG	23	AG	27.6
others	18	others	8.1

[a]Percentage of total vote not obtainable.
[b]6-week delay because of boycott by electoral officials.
[c]Results from one constituency destroyed when jeep bearing them was burned.
SOURCES: Richard L. Sklar and C. S. Whitaker, Jr., "Nigeria" in James S. Coleman

ever, since no office of "Federal Prime Minister" existed for Azikiwe, Nigeria's foremost politician of the day, there were no exceptions to the practice of each main party leader concentrating on political control of his own region. In the federal election of that year, the major contestants were taught a lesson in the im-

1959 Seats	1964 Percent of total vote in region	1964 Seats
21	UPGA	6
33		
	NNA	36
7	other	1
58	UPGA	87[b]
14		
1		
134	NNA	163
7	UPGA	4
25		
8		
2		
1		
	Midwest	
	UPGA	13
		1[c]
134	NNA	197
89	UPGA	108
73	other	5
16		

and Carl G. Rosberg, Jr., eds., *Political Parties and National Integration in Tropical Africa*, Berkeley: University of California Press, 1964, pp. 652–654. Reprinted by permission of The Regents of the University of California. John P. Mackintosh, ed., *Nigerian Government and Politics*, part III.

portance of controlling their own homegrounds as the NCNC upset AG in Western Region. From that time on, Nigerian politics became increasingly monopolized under regional single-party situations.

Regional elections present the best evidence of this development. In 1960, AG won 79 of 122 seats in Western Region Legislature. In the North in 1961, NCP won 160 of 170 seats, and in the East NCNC won 106 of 146 seats. Finally, in the anti-Yoruba Midwest in 1964, NCNC captured 53 of 64 seats. This trend and the split in AG were the contributing elements in the formation of cross-regional coalitions to contest the 1964 federal elections.

By the 1959 federal election, each party was firmly in control of its region; and from that point on, the main contest was over control of the federal government. Table 19 shows the outcome of three federal elections, which generally substantiates the one-party trend perceived from regional elections. Given the tremendous effectiveness of the dominant parties in controlling regional electoral machinery, Akintola's desire to cooperate with NPC by giving up any claim to political influence in the North is quite understandable.

Minority Parties

When the Eastern and Western Regions achieved internal self-government in 1957, (the North followed in 1958), a major political question concerning over 50 percent of Nigerians was solved: Each region was controlled by a dominant political party. Two serious questions remained, however. The issue of how federal powers would be controlled was answered by the formation of a series of electoral coalitions that could provide the requisites of "majority" and "opposition" at the center; and the status of significant minority peoples in each region, which remained an unresolved question.

Legal guarantees of basic minority rights are dealt with elsewhere. While on the subject of political parties, however, we cannot ignore the long list of parties that arose to espouse the "minorities" issue. Up to a point, each minority political party attempted to weaken its two opponents by chipping away at their dominant support in the other regions. AG attempted to win seats in the Eastern Region and form an opposition within

the regional legislature that could embarrass its NCNC government. NCNC meanwhile tried to win seats, or support other
anti-Yoruba elements who would talk out against AG policies in
the Western Region Legislature. Both groups operated in the
North, NCNC through NEPU, and AG by currying favor, especially among Yoruba living north of the Niger River. The
typical demand of a Nigerian minority tribe during the late 1960s
was for creation of a new region which that tribe (or alliance
of small tribes) could control. Naturally the three major tribes
resisted these encroachments whenever they constituted a threat
to their own regions.

In the Middle Belt, with non-Moslems making up nearly one-
third of its population, non-Hausa tribes responded to political
development after 1945 through ethnically based political parties.
The first of these, Birom Progressive Union, emerged in 1945
advocating a "middle belt" region. The more inclusive northern
non-Moslem League arose in 1950, and gave fresh evidence of
the desire for middle belt autonomy. As NPC gained strength in
the North, middle belt cohesion deteriorated. Other minority
tribes, such as Tiv, continued their strong support for the regionalist concept, and by 1958, they had allied with AG as the best
hope for asserting their freedom from Hausa-Fulani control. During the 1960s however, this Tiv-dominated arm of AG, called
United Middle Belt Congress (UMBC), broke with AG and
allied itself with NEPU.[5] Thus, NCNC influence in the Northern
Region was exercised through NEPU, especially in the cities
where Ibo immigrants were concentrated. Bornu Youth Movement was another NCNC ally in the North, but these anti-NPC
alliances failed to win extensive representation once NPC was
organized throughout the region.

In the Eastern Region, anti-Ibo sentiment among smaller
tribes in the southern and eastern sections culminated in the
Calabar-Ogoja Rivers (COR) State Movement following the
1957 regional elections. AG worked with several political parties

[5] For a detailed analysis of one of Nigeria's "minority parties," see J. M.
Dent, "A Minority Party—The United Middle Belt Congress," in Mackintosh, ed., Nigerian Government, pp. 461–508.

to espouse this cause. United National Independence Party
(UNIP), for example, helped AG to capture 10 of the 42 seats
in the 1954 election, and then won 5 seats in the 1957 regional
contest.

Western Region, conversely, witnessed attempted intrusions
from NCNC and NPC into the AG power center. As the 1953
election had shown, NCNC organization in Western Region was
extensive, and capable of exploiting the traditional intra-Yoruba
rivalries. Though its fortunes declined thereafter, alliance with
elements in Western Region still paid dividends for NCNC: An
example is that the party called *Mabolaje* could be counted on to
rally the Ibadan Yoruba against AG. NPC leverage in Western
Region came after independence and culminated in the events
of 1964–1965 described below. As in the case of NCNC intrusion,
the source of NPC influence was intra-Yoruba animosity, particularly the Awolowo-Akintola split.

Finally, the Niger delta area was composed of non-Yoruba
peoꞁ 'es who resented inclusion into Western Region, and it provided a lucrative base of activity for NCNC pressures. The Midwest Front Movement was the NCNC ally that worked for a
separate Midwest Region throughout the late 1950s. In the area's
most important city, NCNC influence was exercised locally
through the Benin-based *Otu Edo*.

The major party which seems to have feared proliferation of
regions the least was AG. Awolowo's party consistently advocated
the transfer of Ilorin (northern) Yoruba to the Western Region
through a boundary adjustment, and the creation of Middle Belt
and COR Regions. By 1960, AG even seemed willing to have
the Midwest carved out of Western Region if the other suggested regions could also be created. The ability of Nigerian
parties to forge continuing national platforms and outlooks was
constantly weakened by the effects of the regional alliance system.
The NCNC's strength, for example,

was derived from a patchwork of local interests and the exploitation
of local prejudices, with a resulting tendency to become involved in
local affairs to the exclusion of broader, national issues. Even in the
Ibo East important branches of the party—particularly those in

Onitsha and Enugu—at times during the 1950's became absorbed in local issues virtually to the exclusion of all else, and these issues in fact tended to affect relations between national leaders of the party.[6]

Electoral Coalitions of 1964–1965

There have been two types of political party organizations that have transcended tribal lines. The first type, the congress or front, included only the significant but progressively diluted NCNC. The second type was the formal electoral coalition within which constituent political parties retained their identity, but cooperated for the purpose of defeating candidates from parties antagonistic to their mutual interests. These coalitions were ordinarily extremely fragile, but they became quite significant after May 1962, when the Western Region Crisis and the controversy over the census strained relations between the partners of the coalition NCNC-NPC Federal Government.

Federal elections were scheduled for December 1964. During the months preceding that fateful election, a complete change of party alignments took place under circumstances which revealed the instability of the system. NCNC leaders were bitter about the revised census, which had produced unexpectedly low figures for the Eastern Region, while upholding the high figures for the Northern Region. NPC, on the other hand, viewed their "partner's" behavior during the general strike of 1964 as two-faced: The coalition had agreed on a government bargaining package only to have NCNC speak out against the government's offer in the East. In July 1964, the Sardauna (Sultan) of the North, Ahmadu Bello, announced, "The Ibos have never been true friends of the North and never will be." [7] NPC then sought alliance with Akintola's faction, which had been put in control of Western Region in 1962. The Nigerian National Alliance (NNA) was formed from NPC and Akintola's NNDP. Also

[6] K. W. Post, "The National Council of Nigeria and the Cameroons, the Decision of December, 1959," in *Ibid.*, p. 410.

[7] Schwarz, *Nigeria*, p. 164.

joining NNA were two Eastern Region minority parties which opposed NCNC there—Niger Delta Congress, which advocated a separate state for delta tribes wary of Ibo domination, and Dynamic Party, a vehicle for the vibrant personality of Dr. Chike Obi, an Ibo mathematician who derided NCNC's unfulfilled promises. That NNA was a marriage of convenience with few policy interests in common is a fact which must have been evident to eastern voters in 1965 who failed to award Dynamic Party a single seat because of its alliance with NNA.

NCNC countered the NPC initiative by making common cause with the Awolowo faction of Yoruba, who represented the majority of that ethnic group; Akintola had never convinced the Yoruba that AG had erred in expelling him, and Awolowo, though still emotionally their leader, languished in jail. United Progressive Grand Alliance (UPGA) was formed from this union of NCNC and AG, and naturally offered a welcome alternative for the opposition parties in the North, NEPU and UMBC. Though the creation of NNA and UPGA as electoral coalitions should not be confused with the creation of a genuine two-party system, it is interesting to speculate on the impact these coalitions might have had on Nigerian politics. In any case, electoral corruption, subsequent military government, and the abolition of the existing political parties put an end to the maneuvering.

Prospects for Party Development During the 1970s

"I have absolutely no fears about the future in any manner, form or shape—provided I am still alive." [8] If the Gowon Regime has its way, nearly 10 years will elapse between the first chaotic epoch of political party development and the resumption of any such activity. Renewed civilian democratic rule is scheduled for 1976, assuming completion of a nine-point program of preparations which the current military regime will direct:

[8] An Ibo respondent quoted by Free, The Attitudes, Hopes and Fears of Nigerians, p. 71.

1. reorganization of the military;
2. completion of Second Development Plan, 1970–1974;
3. eradication of corruption;
4. settlement of the "additional states" issue;
5. agreement on new constitutional structure;
6. agreement on a new revenue allocation formula;
7. a national census;
8. organization of "genuinely national" political parties;
9. holding of elections and selections of governments for federal and state levels.

Chronologically, the Federal Military Council intends the re-emergence of political party organizations to follow points one to seven, steps which would finally settle basic issues that have encouraged the ethnically based parties of the past. It remains to be seen whether this nine-point program will be completed according to schedule, and, if so, whether the impact on subsequent politics will be as intended. In any case, Gowon's view is that "the old political parties were dissolved by decree in 1966. When the time comes, brand new parties . . . will arise." [9]

In part, the political dialogue of the early 1970s seems to substantiate Gowon's hopes for "national" parties. Though the ethnic underpinnings of political factionalism are still important, ideological consciousness and diversity are definitely emerging among Nigerian politicians, who will be the core of any future party system. It is now far more likely that Nigerian politics during the 1970s will lend itself at least partially to analysis according to the familiar concepts of "left" and "right." Domestic and foreign policy issues (to be discussed in Chapters Eight and Nine) will encourage this trend. The probable retention of at least twelve states and possibly more will also lessen the ethnic basis of politics on the federal level. It seems logical that truly national coalitions will be easier to build from the new issues and settings than from those which produced NNA in 1964.

Several of the domestic issues that are likely to encourage

[9] A recent discussion of political prospects for postwar Nigeria is Pauline H. Baker, "The Politics of Nigerian Military Rule," in *Africa Report* 16, no. 2 (February, 1971):18–21; and A. Bolaji Akinyemi, "Nigeria: What Should Follow Army Rule and When," in *Ibid.*, pp. 22–23.

ideological rather than ethnic arguments have arisen since the civil war began. Though political parties may not be allowed until 1974, the ideological nuclei are already appearing. The right of the political spectrum includes some of the higher civil servants who are the foundation of Federal Military Government. The Chief of State, General Gowon, seems to speak most frequently for this group, which is oriented toward (1) retaining the present twelve-state structure which they have built and will defend; (2) encouraging foreign investment by reassurances that no hasty nationalization will be carried out; and (3) resisting a completely "free national education" plan and any other domestic schemes which they deem fiscally irresponsible.

Nigeria's "right" is composed principally of the expanding business community which will grow stronger if the impressive postwar economic growth continues. This sector lacks strong, popular political leadership, however, and concentrates more on specific concerns, such as obtaining governmental loan support. Given strong leadership in the future, the numerous small commercial traders could become allied to a more conservative-moderate political party, especially if the "socialism" of Awolowo and others appears as a fundamental threat to their way of life. However, we should recall from Chapter Six that in the past this group played a role as support for one of the ethnically-oriented dominant southern parties, and was therefore more willing to support the aims of other Ibo (for example) than to support traders from other tribes.

Nigeria's "left" is developing mostly from a composite of university, labor, and bureaucratic elements. The present government seems generally oriented to the left of the prewar regime, and even Gowon's surface "conservatism" may be more the product of pragmatic caution then ideology. While the military-bureaucratic leadership would not welcome any further drastic fractionalizing of Nigeria's twelve-state system, neither would they accept a return to a confederal system as weak as that of the First Republic. Statements in the Second National Development Plan make this clear. Nigeria, the plan argues, is a developing country which operates in "a state of permanent crisis hardly distinguishable in its essence from war-time mobilization." [10] Its specific allocations demonstrate, as the next chapter will outline, greater economic centralization than ever before.

The economist, Dr. S. Aluko, has spoken vigorously against foreign monopoly and over-generous concessions to the oil companies, and similar sentiment emanates regularly from the universities. But the best known Nigerian on the left side of the political spectrum is Awolowo, Federal Commissioner for Finance from 1967–1971. By the time politics formally resumes, however, younger men may oppose "Awo," who will be 67 in 1976, the year elections are promised. Nevertheless, Awolowo's impact through his writings, particularly his most recent works, is impressive and far-reaching. His economic and social vocabulary is "socialist," but not rashly so; his statements on nationalization have less bite than those of Aluko, for example. Awo is also more moderate than the former Federal Commissioner for Economic Affairs, Alhaji Gusau, who resigned in 1970 in protest against the "conservative" governmental policies. It is quite possible that a leftist political organization could emerge from all of these elements, including also the Federal Commissioner of Communications, Alhaji Aminu Kano and the Union Leader, Wahaab Goodluck, who appears to be the most "radical leftist" of the leaders mentioned above.

More than the "right," Nigeria's new "left" is cross-tribal to a remarkable degree, and may become impressively effective as a molder of a "Nigerian" orientation to political issues. Common purposes potentially bind northerners (Gasau, Kano) Yoruba (Awolowo) and many Ibo. For the more politically conscious Ibo, a turn to the left would be understandable under the successive circumstances of humiliating defeat, unemployment, and resentment against the Rivers State for the loss of their property in the city of Port Harcourt.

Another issue which may go far to crystallize the Nigerian left is the timetable for the return to politics. Awolowo, for example,

[10] Ministry of Economic Development, Government of Nigeria, *Second National Development Plan: 1970–1974*. Lagos: Nigerian National Press, 1970.

surely hopes for political activity before 1976 and has specifically disagreed with Gowon on the nature of the constituent assembly. Gowon conceives of a nominated assembly which will consider a draft constitution, while Awolowo favors census and elected assembly preceding the new constitution, thereby lending greater legitimacy to it. Mass support for this coalition would follow from workers who have long been throttled by the antistrike Decree #53, renewed in 1970, and from the swelling ranks of unemployed. This mass support would come as no surprise to social scientists who have studied Nigeria. As early as 1964, Lloyd Free wrote:

[S]hould a feeling of collective frustration and pessimism develop about the national front, it might spill over into a mood of individual frustration, pessimism and despair at the personal level. This, in turn, might make radical political appeals much more attractive to the Nigerian people than they are now.[11]

Finally, Nigeria's intelligentsia would find the move to the left a natural culmination of their critical role during their country's first turbulent decade. Lekan Balogun is one example of many Nigerian social scientists who advocate uncompromising socialism and centralism.[12] These intellectuals have had enough of tribalism and its effects, and are vocal enough to command an audience.

The intelligentsia are also disgusted with corruption, but it is impossible to predict whether the Nigerian people will follow politicians who make corruption a key issue. There is no recent interview data to suggest relevant attitude trends, but a decade ago during the height of the Western Region trials, only 16 percent of a sample of Nigerians mentioned "dishonest government or leaders" as a major fear. The survey director, Lloyd Free, concluded that "the relatively low frequency of mentions of dishonest government supports the impression, gained by the writer on the spot, that many Nigerians take a reasonable amount of graft and corruption for granted."[13]

11 Free, *The Attitudes, Hopes and Fears of Nigerians*, p. 71.
12 Lekan Balogun, *Nigeria: Social Justice or Doom*, Ibadan: Yemesi Publications, 1970.
13 Free, *The Attitudes, Hopes and Fears of Nigerians*, p. 44. To balance his conclusion, Free does point out that the Nigerians' exposure to corruption was very high compared to other countries surveyed.

CHAPTER EIGHT

Development Plans
and Policy Dilemmas

YOUNG AMERICANS are accustomed to questioning what one recent text has labeled the "perverted priorities" of our system. In our rush towards the highest living standard the world has ever seen, we have produced many problems which now plague our society and becloud our sense of purpose. Our leaders debate even our most basic goals. Should we go to the planets, or clean up our cities? Should we spur greater economic development, or concentrate on improving the quality of life? It is not difficult for us, through study of our own economic and political history, to sense that the very growth processes that brought on our ambivalent situation were neither anticipated nor planned.

To understand what is perhaps the most fundamental difference between the "desire to plan" in most new countries like Nigeria, and the haphazard development of our own land, students must grasp the different economic assumptions of two epochs. Economic changes in Western countries, triggered by the Renaissance, the Reformation, and the Industrial Revolution, transformed traditional society, yet there were no models or strategies to serve as the basis for rapid growth and expansion. The prevalent political theories espoused by the elite were compatible with the laissez-faire economics of the day. It is easy to see, in retrospect, how these conditions have been misrepresented as "special cases" of economic development without government influence. There was, in fact, a considerable role for government to play in the economic development of the United States, Britain, and the other presently developed countries. In our case, the government provided land and protected the developing economy and changing society from various foreign and frontier enemies. The British government controlled the seas, providing ideal conditions for economic expansion without the costs of land empire.

Nigeria is typical of a throng of new countries which have emerged during an era when the world's eyes are focused on the lifestyle of the most wealthy nations. Furthermore, as former colonies, most new countries have abnormally close links with an industrial nation through their educated elite.

While the United States does not set out long range "plans" in the same sense as most other countries, we do recognize the importance of keeping adequate statistics on key indicators of the nation's economic and social development, and of correcting imbalances that may indicate serious problems. Some of the world's developed countries go further: France's Sixth Plan (1970–1974) is a comprehensive attempt to promote desired rates of growth, while bringing certain sectors into line with Common Market guidelines. The Soviet Union, and Communist countries generally, place a heavy emphasis on control over economic progress, achieved in part through planning. Through a composite socioeconomic index, Table 6 (page 80) demonstrated the overall backwardness of Nigeria. A study of the detailed categories that compose that index, such as income levels, education, and mass media development, would indicate more specifically that Nigeria is a desperately underdeveloped country in comparison to the United States.

Americans who automatically condemn leaders of a country like Nigeria for rushing headlong into "communist style" control over the economy and society through planning, have perhaps not adequately understood the uniqueness of our own experience. Although stopping short of pure economic determinism, the late historian David Potter pointed out that the American political style is closely related, through cause and effect, to our unique economic abundance. Our basic democratic tenets of mobility and achieved status were viable "because an economic surplus was available to pay democracy's promissory notes." [1] In short, our people's expectations from our political system were realizable, even though these goals were more materialistic than those of any previous society. Potter argues that a glance at a listing of American involvement in world affairs will show our dichotomized definition of political systems. We define "democracy" in terms of our own practice of that form of government in our own unique situation, and thus assume that socialism does not qualify as "democracy" because its exact treatment of its citizens reflects a different mixture of liberty and welfare. Our ideals have, in Potter's words,

caused us to hope falsely that other countries will embrace democracy as we understand it, and to misconstrue badly the reasons for their failure to do so. It has even led us to condemn, quite unjustly, the countries which fail to establish a democracy like our own, as if it were plain obstinacy or even outright iniquity which explains their behavior.[2]

Therefore, we have no reason to censure Nigerian attempts to employ all means at their disposal to ensure economic and social development. Our preaching the assets of free market economy appears irrelevant to leaders in a less developed country. Robert Heilbroner's allegorical account of "market-oriented" advisors in a new country makes this point well.

We could imagine the leaders of such a nation saying, "We have always experienced a highly tradition-bound way of life. Our men hunt and cultivate the fields and perform the tasks as they are brought up to do by the force of example and the instruction of their elders. We know, too, something of what can be done by economic command. We are prepared, if necessary, to sign an edict making it compulsory for many of our men to work on community projects for our national development. Tell us, is there any other way we can organize our society so that it will function successfully—or better yet, more successfully?"

Suppose we answered, "Yes, there is another way. Organize your society along the lines of a market economy."

[1] David M. Potter, *People of Plenty*, Chicago: University of Chicago Press, 1954, p. 93.
[2] *Ibid.*, p. 112.

"Very well," say the leaders. "What do we then tell people to do? How do we assign them to their various tasks?"

"That's the very point," we would answer. "In a market economy no one is assigned to any task. The very idea of a market society is that each person is allowed to decide for himself what to do."

There is consternation among the leaders. "You mean there is no assignment of some men to mining and others to cattle raising? No manner of selecting some for transportation and others for cloth weaving? You leave this to people to decide for themselves? But what happens if they do not decide correctly? What happens if no one volunteers to go into the mines, or if no one offers himself as a railway engineer?"

"You may rest assured," we tell the leaders, "none of that will happen. In a market society, all the jobs will be filled because it will be to people's advantage to fill them."

Our respondents accept this with uncertain expression. "Now look," one of them finally says, "let us suppose that we take your advice and let people do as they please. Now let's talk about something important, like cloth production. Just how do we fix the right level of cloth output in the 'market society' of yours?"

"But you don't," we reply.

"We don't! Then how do we know there will be enough cloth produced?"

"There will be," we tell him. "The market will see to that."

"Then how do we know there won't be too much cloth produced?" he asks triumphantly.

"Ah, but the market will see to that too!"

"But what is this market that will do all these wonderful things? Who runs it?"

"Oh, nobody runs the market," we answer. "It runs itself. In fact, there isn't really any such thing as 'the market.' It's just a word we use to describe the way people behave."

"But I thought people behave the way they wanted to!"

"And so they do," we say. "But never fear. They will want to behave the way you want them to behave."

"I am afraid," says the chief of the delegation, "that we are wasting our time. We thought you had in mind a serious proposal. . . ."[3]

Nigerian leaders have expressed since before independence their firm desire to be in control of their national economic development and social change. For Awolowo, success in his post as

[3] Robert L. Heilbroner, The Making of Economic Society, Englewood Cliffs, N.J.: Prentice-Hall, 3d ed., 1970, pp. 14–15.

Western Region Premier from 1951–1959 meant cementing four freedoms for his people: political independence, and freedom from ignorance, disease, and poverty. After 1960, as before, Awolowo recognized that these socioeconomic challenges faced Nigeria's leadership with "towering problems of an intractable character." [4] Though his political views were very different from those of Awolowo, Sir Ahmadu Bello echoed the Yoruba leader's sentiment on the need for development.

There is so much to be done to develop this country that sometimes it leaves me quite dismayed. As I drive along the roads and see the simple villagers in their farms, I see what a lot there is to be done to raise the standard of these good people to what it should be. I see the men working in their farms with the same kind of hoe that their fathers and their grandfathers used before them. They are bent double over their work in the blazing sunshine and their wives and children come and help them. What can we do to make things easier?[5]

The socialist Awolowo, as aware as his northern counterpart of the developmental deficiencies of his country, was perhaps more willing to support government-sponsored action. He saw that it was "urgent and imperative that we should plan on a much bolder and grander scale." [6]

People join their leaders in assuming that government will take the lead in providing a better life. The psychologist, Lloyd Free, who directed the Nigerian survey for *The Patterns of Human Concerns*, was surprised by the connection made by Nigerians between personal and national concerns. Individual and family problems are "also considered national problems, about which government is expected to do something. They thus have *political* significance." Free surmised that this habit derived from people becoming accustomed to the central role of the colonial government. The new national government had simply inherited this role.[7]

[4] Chief Obafemi Awolowo, *Awo: The Autobiography of Chief Obafemi Awolowo*, London: Cambridge University Press, 1960, p. 256. See also ch. 15.

[5] Sir Ahmadu Bello, *My Life*, London: Cambridge University Press, 1962, p. 237.

[6] Awolowo, *Awo*, p. 315.

[7] Free, *The Attitudes, Hopes and Fears of Nigerians*, pp. 37–39.

Ironically, experience in Nigeria and other less developed countries shows that planning has been comparatively ineffective. There are many reasons which may account for this: (1) lack of adequate data with which to judge the starting points and strategies of development; (2) events that have diverted attention from the planning task; (3) disputes over priorities and revenue sources, coupled with general ignorance and apathy, which limit the peoples' commitment to carry out projects; (4) failure of proposed revenue sources; (5) excessive optimism of political leaders. A development plan is a series of targets set up in various economic fields, but it is the success of actual projects—the increased production of crops and industries—that determines whether the goals in a plan will be met. Without the will to force the people to implement the plan, through a dictatorial political system, leaders have no assurance of meeting projected goals.

In fact, the economic planners of independent Nigeria began their work with no illusions about any "miracles" that a National Development Plan might produce. Recognizing that the shortage of accurate data was a serious detriment to precise planning, Professor Wolfgang Stolper, who headed the team of economists responsible for Nigeria's first National Development Plan, 1962–1968, cited five possible remedies.

1. Collection of data in all areas relevant to development should be one of the plan's targets.
2. Plan goals should be as modest as the "framework of known facts, legal and social surroundings, and executive abilities" indicated.
3. Progress assessment takes time, and small projects are as easy to assess as big ones, and at less possible net cost.
4. Decision-making must be "decentralized and delegated" to allow local initiatives to make up for inadequate information.
5. Planning must not be pursued rigidly.[8]

Obviously, Stolper was not sympathetic toward vigorous central planning. His perception of Nigerian postindependence politics led him to conclude that mere rhetoric from leaders about the

8 Wolfgang F. Stolper, Planning Without Facts, Cambridge, Mass.: Harvard University Press, 1966, pp. 11–14, and ch. 1.

needs for development should not be mistaken for willingness to make sacrifices for the sake of coordinated planning. "It may well be that economic development has not, in fact, the high priority in the thinking and aspirations of the people or even of the leaders of underdeveloped countries as these leaders pretend." [9] The realities of Nigerian politics did not elude Stolper, who no doubt realized that of the four governments involved in carrying out the proposed plan, two at most would be firmly committed to its implimentation. With the formation of Midwest Region, and the ouster of Awolowo from his position of power in Western Region politics, only Dr. Okpara's Eastern Region government was sympathetic to the idea. In his comparison of four African development plans, R. H. Green referred to the natural tendency of a government to

select an economist whom it believes to have an outlook in at least general accord with its own. Nigeria's conservative government, made up of and backed by men with interests in private business and public contracts, employed Professor Stolper, whose basic preferences, in accord with their own, were for private enterprise in directly productive sectors, supported by large scale state investment in infrastructure, and against policies of austerity and income redistribution." [10]

The result, argued Green, was a weak plan unlikely to spur even the modest overall growth rate of 4 percent which it projected. During the First Republic there were some Nigerians, both academicians and bureaucrats, among them Dr. Pius Okigbo, then President of the Nigerian Economic Society, who thought much more could have been accomplished, but they were not in positions to control the planning process. Men less favorable to planning, such as Finance Minister Chief Festus Okotie-Eboh, were in power, and consequently there was a lack of coordination between federal and regional Plans, encouraged by the weakness of the National Economic Council and the Federal Ministry of Economic Development.

Economic policies have changed considerably since 1966. An

[9] *Ibid.*, p. 16.
[10] Reginald H. Green, "Four African Development Plans," *Journal of Modern African Studies* 3, no. 2 (August, 1965):260.

indication of the more vigorous role central government is to play appeared as early as June 1966 in *Guideposts for Second National Development Plan*, which openly hinted at the inadequacy of the 1962–1968 Plan. The document cited "a great need to re-examine the whole basis of our planning efforts," and called for a new Plan "designed as part of a total strategy for social transformation and (as) a deliberate tool of social change." [11] Despite the ouster of the Ironsi regime by more conservative officers shortly after these statements were made, it is obvious from the nature of the new Plan, published in November 1970, that during the intervening years of civil war, two factors have led to the retention of Ironsi's desire to centralize economic policy. Firstly, the role of Nigerians in bureaucratic offices, and in important advisory positions (such as the National Economic Planning Advisory Group) has increased the nationalistic flavor of economic thought. Conservative and/or business-oriented leaders of the First Republic, such as the Northern and Western Regional and Federal Prime Ministers and the Federal Minister of Finance, have lost power along with the expatriate economic advisors they hired. In place of these came supporters of Awolowo, who served as Minister of Finance from 1967–1971.

The second centralizing influence has been the civil war itself. The Federal Military Government became accustomed to "directing" domestic policy generally, and does not appear willing to defer to the wishes of twelve state governments just because Biafra has been defeated. The *Second National Development Plan* argues, in fact, for a continued strong role for the center, citing Nigeria's condition as typical of many underdeveloped countries which face a self-defined "crisis." [12] The remainder of this chapter will examine several key domestic policy areas to see the extent of this new and apparently vigorous trend of economic

[11] Republic of Nigeria, *Guideposts for Second National Development Plan*, Lagos: Ministry of Economic Development, June, 1966, p. 1.

[12] Republic of Nigeria, *Second National Development Plan, 1970–1974*, p. 31. For a sample of the thought which contributed to the "Second Plan," see Nigerian Institute of Social and Economic Research, "Conference on National Reconstruction and Development in Nigeria" (Papers and Proceedings), March 24–29, 1969 (Ibadan: N.I.S.E.R., 1969).

nationalism that makes Nigeria of the 1970s so different from the First Republic.

Industrial Development

The Second National Development Plan allocates $658 million for specific long-term industrial development projects, of which $114 million are to be spent during 1970–1974. These planned projects include oil, gas, and petrochemical refineries, three auto assembly plants, and an iron and steel complex. These figures may not seem impressive for a nation of over 60 million people, and even the total investment for all sectors encompassed by the plan, $4.5 billion, pales in comparison to our own government's investment totals; but this is primarily a result of limited resources. A more adequate indicator of Nigeria's new outlook is the approach government takes towards control over economic resources and activity.

Since the postwar era began, familiar calls have been heard · for foreign investment. Full-page spreads in The New York Times, the Economist, and other media advertise Nigeria's fruitful investment climate. Scratch the surface of these open-armed invitations, and warnings against unrestrained business activity are quick to appear. The Federal Commissioner of Trade and Industry warned in a March 1970 speech that Nigeria now expects from foreign and domestic businessmen "genuine co-operation and partnership," adding: "We have had too much in the past of machine salesmen who promoted dubiously conceived industrial projects in this country."[13] In a similar vein, General Gowon, in his budget speech for 1970–1971, indicated that external assistance for the new Plan was welcomed "as a whole." He quickly added:

But we would like to serve notice to all those who can assist our development effort that we shall welcome only the external assistance that can be promptly utilized in the appropriate phases of the recon-

[13] S. H. Monguno, Federal Commissioner for Trade and Industries, "Government and the Investor," speech to Second National Conference of the Association of Chambers of Commerce, Industries and Mines, Kano, Nigeria, March 21, 1970, pp. 7, 8.

struction programme. Assistance in the form of programme support of general commodity loan will be more valuable than protracted and endless negotiations over individual projects as in the past. We are no longer interested in external donors who spend all their time on publicizing their aid activities in Nigeria without doing anything concrete to really assist our development effort on the ground.[14]

The most striking evidence of Nigeria's new economic nationalism is her much changed attitude toward oil resources. Foreign oil drillers have until recently benefitted from generous terms of profit repatriation. Nigeria shares, with Libya, two main advantages over other oil producing states—comparatively short hauling distances to Europe and the United States (much Middle Eastern oil is shipped around Africa since the 1967 closing of Suez), and low sulphur content (less conducive to pollution). In 1969, the government intention to extend greater command over the petroleum industry became obvious with legal control over drilling concessions. Nigeria had been claiming well below 50 percent of the gross revenues, but during 1970–1971, after watching the negotiations between oil companies and OPEC (Organization of Petroleum Exporting Countries) the government has taken a consistently tougher stand. The new Development Plan calls for a government share of 55 percent of the revenues in important industries. Discussions beginning in March 1971, will decide the precise agreements about oil prices and revenues, but Nigeria does seem headed toward the more militant views held by OPEC countries.[15]

The effects which Nigeria's petroleum may have on her general development program raise complex issues. The potential impact is obvious. It is estimated that by 1973, this industry may be providing 50 percent of all government revenues, and 11 percent of the total projected GNP. Experience reveals that oil producing

[14] H. E. The Head of the Federal Military Government and Commander-in-Chief of the Armed Forces, Major-General Yakubu Gowon, "Building a Great and Happier Nation," National Budget Broadcast (1970–1971), p. 9.
[15] Economist Intelligence Unit, Quarterly Economic Review: Nigeria, no. 2, April 7, 1971.

countries have varied greatly in their use of revenues on such a scale. In some cases, sheiks' pockets have been filled while the peasants' life continues as before. Since the oil industry requires a large proportion of equipment, technology, and skills, and very little untrained manpower, the benefits of oil revenues are not likely to be direct. Furthermore, this is not the type of industry that will furnish a market for goods produced by other Nigerian enterprises, or otherwise stimulate the economy through "linkage effects." Benefits from the fabulous growth potential of Nigerian oil will more likely be indirect; revenues will most likely be used for other development projects unrelated to oil.[16]

These industrial development considerations lead to two other political issues: nationalization, and budget allocations between federal and state governments. On the first issue, the move to the left in Nigerian policy making seems to have progressed to the point where nationalization is a serious threat. The 4-year-old development plan includes promises that no program of "indiscriminate nationalization" will occur. It is obvious, however, that the Nigerian government intends to establish a new measure of control over foreign firms to make sure resource extraction reflects the country's needs. Companies are to proceed as fast as possible with "Nigerianization"; the training and promotion of indigenous replacements for expatriate employees. Further, the Plan calls for a "radical and militant program of social action" to transform Nigerian society.[17]

A trend toward nationalism of foreign capital should not be automatically confused with "socialism." The Nigerians seem to be still committed to the idea of a vigorous indigenous private

[16] Scott R. and Sandra C. Pearson, "Oil Boom Reshapes Nigeria's Future," *Africa Report* 16, no. 2 (February, 1971): 14–17. See also Scott R. Pearson, *Petroleum and the Nigerian Economy*, Stanford, Calif.: Stanford University Press, 1970, ch. X. Pearson's argument advises the Nigerian government to maximize oil exports, and profits, by continuing the private foreign investment system, which encourages the most foreign interest. Threats of nationalization since 1970 indicate that Nigeria is moving in the opposite direction. Also, see Ludwig H. Schätzl, *Petroleum in Nigeria*, Ibadan: Oxford University Press, 1969.

[17] *Second National Development Plan, 1970–1974*, p. 31.

economic sector, even in the face of conditions which make a
successful business start more difficult than, say, for an American
in our economy.[18]

The other key political issue, budget allocations, shows the
increasing trend of the federal government toward dominance
over the states. Since Nigerian politics awakened in force after
World War II, the argument over how revenues should be ap-
portioned had been increasingly solved in favor of the richer
regions. Before the massive discoveries of oil (mostly located in
the southeast and delta areas), Eastern Region was the chief
exponent of allocation by "need" (meaning the collection at the
center of revenues derived in regions and their reallocation based
on the merit of proposed expenses). The richer North and West
had favored the concept of "derivation," allocation according to
the revenues collected in each region.

Since the Biafran war, the Federal Military Government has
begun to express its views on this important issue. According to
General Gowon, "The Federal Government is committed to
giving financial assistance to needy States to enable them to stand
on their own feet and play an effective role in the task of nation-
building." [19] Furthermore, a 1969 study commission recommended
revenue allocation based heavily on the principle of need. Presently, 40 percent of revenues (except from oil) go toward allocations
from the center, while 60 percent remain in the state in which
they were collected. (By the end of 1970, 45 percent of oil revenues went to the states and 55 percent to the center, where an
elaborate compromise governed their allocation to projects in the
states.) This situation represented an improvement on prewar
formulas based on the principle of derivation. However, it still
implied that the richer states, in particular Rivers State with its
concentration of oil, would continue to grow even more wealthy
than the more populous East Central State, or the resource-poor
Kwara State. A new commission on budget allocations was to

[18] Sayre P. Schatz, "The High Cost of Aiding Business in Developing
Economies: Nigeria's Loans Programs," Oxford Economic Papers XX, no. 3
(November, 1968):427–434.
[19] Gowon, "Building a Great and Happier Nation," p. 5.

study the problem during 1971, and the trend toward allocations based on need seemed likely to intensify, with each state receiving downwards of one-fifth of the oil profits produced within its borders.[20]

Agricultural Development

Nigerian planners seem increasingly conscious of the importance of improvement in agricultural development. Between 70 and 80 percent of the national workforce are farmers, and recent changes in economic thinking have seemingly had an impact on Nigerian agricultural planning. The shifts in economic development theory toward stressing agriculture's role are typified by the transformation of the well-known economist, Gunnar Myrdal. In *An International Economy* (1956) Myrdal echoed the accepted doctrine of that decade; the agricultural sector contains too many "human factors" which can destroy the impact of the economist's analyses of economic data. Of course, at that time it appeared that intensive capital emphasis on industry was not only theoretically desirable, but also monetarily feasible. Britain, France, the United States, and the Soviet Union appeared committed, for a variety of reasons, to subsidizing an expensive approach toward development. By the 1970s, this picture had changed considerably. Foreign aid had reached neither the qualitative nor quantitative levels hoped for; and the economists meanwhile realized the error of ignoring agriculture. Myrdal's *Asian Drama* (1968) stressed agricultural productivity.

Finally, Nigerian agencies cooperated with American universities in a study which concluded that "rural transormation is the key to growth and development of Nigeria, 1969–1985."[21] There

[20] "Nigeria Starts Again: A Survey," *The Economist*, October 24, 1970, xv. For a detailed discussion of this subject, see O. Teriba, "Nigerian Revenue Allocation Experience, 1952–1965: A Study in Intergovernmental Fiscal and Financial Relations," *Nigerian Journal of Economic and Social Studies* VIII, no. 3 (November, 1966):361–382.

[21] W. M. Myers, "Aid in a new format," *Africa Report*, May, 1970, p. 30.

are indications of the government's concern for agriculture, which, until oil's rapid growth, provided two-thirds of Nigerian exports.[22]

The new Nigerian Plan allocates 12.9 percent of government investment to agriculture. An arrangement with Ford and Rockefeller Foundations resulted in an Agricultural Research Institute, which began operations in Spring 1970.

Nigerian economists are still, however, concerned that their growing consensus has not filtered through to the policymakers. One academician insists that "at this stage of Nigerian economic development, an improved agriculture is essential to industrial development. Lip service is often paid to the importance of agriculture, but it is commonly believed that industrialization holds the key to increased national wealth." [23] Properly used, the oil revenues could stimulate agriculture by subsidizing marketing boards. Farmers would receive higher prices for their crops, or would pay lower taxes. Stimulating the agricultural sector in this way would also lessen undesirable urban migration.

Within the agricultural sector itself, policy alternatives reflect a similar type of controversy. The choice between industry and agriculture can be equated to the argument among agriculturalists about whether to improve existing farm patterns or replace them with more modern arrangements. In 1959, "farm settlements" were established in Western Region, and later in other regions. These were small-scale projects involving mechanized techniques and relatively large amounts of capital, designed for greater per acre productivity. Expected advantages were increased employment and profit-yielding innovations that surrounding traditional farmers would learn. As it turned out, farmers resented the expropriation of land for the "farm settlements," regarding them as alien institutions, and were unimpressed by (and unaware of) the technical advances there. Government will have to make

[22] Consortium for the Study of Nigerian Rural Development, *Strategies and Recommendations for Nigerian Rural Development, 1969–1985.* (CSNRD Paper #33) East Lansing, Mich.: Michigan State University Press, July, 1969.

[23] H. A. Oluwasanmi, *Agriculture and Nigerian Economic Development,* Ibadan: Oxford University Press, 1966, p. v. See also ch. 10.

greater efforts to educate farmers toward these projects, for they obviously have the potential to backfire politically.[24]

Social Development

As Nigeria tackles her avowed aim of constructing a just society, a residue of haunting social and educational problems will have to be confronted. For example, the promises made by politicians seeking support for the nationalist effort against domestic opponents led masses of Nigerians to expect universal primary education (UPE).

In the first few years of independence, great sums were spent on mass primary education; but the results were less than expected. By 1966, argues one expert, nearly 70 percent of the populace was still untouched by any educational experience. Furthermore, regional imbalances were unaffected; 62 percent of Eastern Region primary-school-age children were receiving instruction as opposed to 8 percent in the North.[25]

For those who were affected by this assault on ignorance, the humanities-oriented content of Nigerian primary education and the emphasis on masses of graduates has understandably produced an unemployment problem of great magnitude, especially since 1960.[26] Remedies have been considered: UNESCO programs indicate that "functional literacy" can be created at far less expense than through a typical UPE program. The products of such a program may be much more economically sensible than those of the more traditional concept. Primary school is usually enough to convince peasantry that there is something more exciting in

[24] R. O. Abegboye, A. C. Basu, and Dupe Olatunbosun, "Impact of Western Nigerian Farm Settlements on Surrounding Farmers," *Nigerian Journal of Economic and Social Studies* XI, no. 2 (July, 1969):229–240.

[25] Archibald Callaway, "Expanding Nigeria's Education: Projections and Achievements Since Independence," *Nigerian Journal of Economic and Social Studies* XI, no. 2 (July, 1969):191–203.

[26] Ayo Ogunsheye, "Nigeria," in Coleman, ed., *Education and Political Development*, p. 143.

store than farm life, but it is inadequate to prepare them occupationally.[27]

In spite of much evidence that Nigerians are aware of this problem, the advocates of UPE are still committed to spreading their cause, and they are supported by the popular Awolowo. In his latest book, Awolowo makes the strongest case yet for UPE, in association with free secondary and university education, saying that these programs are not only desirable, but financially feasible. Awolowo's proposals would cost nearly $250 million during the 4-year plan alone, but would, he projects, redress the educational imbalance between North and South by 1980.[28] His plans promote an unusual degree of unity among the Nigerian "left," but are condemned as impossibly expensive by many higher civil servants and by more conservative members of the Federal Military Government, including Gowon. Oil revenues may make it possible to finance both UPE and neglected areas of technical and managerial education. Many Nigerians are concerned because in spite of "Nigerianization" efforts, more expatriates work in Nigeria now than in 1960, as a result of high-level manpower shortages.[29]

Nigeria's goal of fully utilizing its human resources will not simply depend on these decisions on UPE, free higher education, and on the total amounts budgeted for these programs. Under the previous educational system, regionalization of the curriculum reduced the effectiveness of schooling as a builder of "Nigerian" attitudes, and unless the new constitutional provisions place ultimate power over curriculum and budget at the center, rather than in the states, a new set of imbalances and localism may arise. Heated argument over these questions is now thriving. At least it is no longer necessary to conclude, as Alan Peshkin did in 1967: "National leaders willing and able to provide the sustenance for [Nigerian unity's] survival appear absent, and,

[27] *Christian Science Monitor*, December 7, 1964, p. 14.
[28] Obafemi, Awolowo, *The Strategy and Tactics of the People's Republic of Nigeria*, New York: Macmillan, 1970.
[29] T. M. Yesufu, *Manpower Problems and Economic Development in Nigeria*, Ibadan: Oxford University Press, 1969.

without such leadership, the schools are mostly important in promoting goals of national unity." [30]

Many other social problems could be discussed in this section to elucidate the difficulties of federal system of government in a setting which requires coordination, and of the need for highly trained manpower among a people who long for mass primary education. One final example will suffice. As previously discussed, Nigerian leaders consider disease and nutrition one of their country's major development crises. After 1951, responsibilities for health devolved to regional, and then in 1967, to state governments, each of which has a Ministry of Health. A National Council for Health coordinates for the Federal Ministry of Health all interstate matters, such as quarantine decisions. But as the former Chief Medical Advisor to the Federal Government indicated, in 1970, devolution of responsibility accentuated the "shortage of manpower at all professional levels, especially to serve the need in the vast and remote rural areas." [31] These requirements seem virtually unattainable; a fourfold increase over the present 2000 doctors by 1980 would be necessary just to attain World Health Organization minimum standards of a 1 to 10,000 doctor to population ratio. Efficient annual production of 600 doctors and their just allocation to rural areas will require a degree of coordination which may test the federalized administrative concept.

Conclusion

The new spirit of economic nationalism and self-reliance in Nigeria is supported by the swing to the left in Nigerian politics, and by a marked distrust of foreigners, especially those who were not decidedly committed to the Federal cause during Nigeria's civil war. General Gowon's stated intention is to preside over the

[30] Alan Peshkin, "Education and National Integration in Nigeria," *Journal of Modern African Studies* 5, no. 3 (November, 1967):334.

[31] Sir Samuel Manuwa, M.D., "A Short Note on Recent Developments in Health Activities in Nigeria," *Bulletin of the American College of Physicians* 11, no. 4 (April, 1970):182.

beginning of the building of "a great and dynamic economy which will be the pride of the black man wherever he may be." [32] This typifies the new sense of purpose which is long overdue, since serious social difficulties emerged during the First Republic and were compounded by neglect during the war. An era of reconstruction faces a country already plagued by agrarian tumult, labor agitation, unemployment, inflation, malaise among the intelligentsia, and the retention of ethnic identities. As late as January 1971, a New York Times correspondent said of Ibo attitudes toward their former exiled leader, Odumegwu Ojukwu, "People still regard him as their leader and they are eager to read about him." [33]

Reconstruction from war's rigors sometimes has its good aspects, however, in that traditional organizations are weakened, mobilization and developmental structures strengthened, and technology is stimulated.[34] Even such a violent and demographically costly conflict seems to have left some positive effects, as the Federal Commissioner for Trade and Industry announced in March 1970: "Despite the tragedies . . . there is no doubt that on the whole the Civil War has had a very positive impact on industry in this country." [35] Production was stimulated in the 90 percent of the country not directly subjected to military operations, and consumer imports were restricted. Nigeria did not incur serious foreign debts, and the basis for sound economic reconstruction and consequent development is unmistakably present.

One of Nigeria's main domestic concerns is the postwar role of the military, which had expanded to a quarter of a million men by 1970. The soldiers are proud, sometimes arrogant in the absence of a strong civilian political mechanism to administer re-

---

[32] H. E. Yakubu Gowon, "Building a Great and Happier Nation," p. 5.

[33] William Borders, in The New York Times, January 17, 1971.

[34] Fred S. Siebert, Theodore Patterson, and Wilbur Schramm, Four Stimulant of Political Development," Comparative Political Studies 3, no. 4 (January, 1971):413–423. Popper does limit his thesis, however. "But if the level of violence becomes too high—as it has in South Vietnam, Biafra, Laos, Cambodia, the Congo, and Algeria, where whole villages have been systemmatically wiped out—then internal war will block development." [Italic mine.]

[35] Monguno, "Government and the Investor," p. 3.

straints. Demobilization is difficult enough in a country that pays soldiers less than a competitive wage. In Nigeria, like most under-developed countries, soldiers are paid more than most people could ever hope to earn. In 1970, the lowest pay rank (private) was receiving $40 a month, which exceeds Nigeria's monthly per capita income by eight times![36] In a country known for its people's concern for individual prospects for status and advancement, this situation is surely intolerable in the long run. *The Patterns of Human Concerns* attitude survey in 1962 found "a widespread feeling of injustice and unfairness in the workings of the Nigerian system" especially in the southern areas. The 23 percent of Nigerians who stressed their anxiety over these evils constituted "by far the highest such figures we have ever encountered in our studies." [37] Demobilization of a force which had achieved one of the rare military victories since World War II is risky, to say the least. Postwar disturbances among wounded veterans indicate the need for policies, some of which may be met by a new Armed Forces Pensions Board. As a prelude to policies which will hope-fully find a legitimate place for Nigeria's Postwar military, an army census was begun in 1971.

The problem of the army's role must be settled quickly for urban reconstruction to begin. (Lagos, which may exceed 5,000,000 by 1975, includes one of the world's worst slums.) Nigeria's level of urbanization is high compared to her level of economic develop-ment. Britain, for example, is 12 times as wealthy, but only 4 times as urbanized as Nigeria's 19 percent in towns over 5000 (1952 census). The result is seen as a "substantial drag on the rate of economic development in the country." Nigeria's over-urbanization is an unhealthy sign for two reasons: it is caused more by the lure of cities than by "push" from rural areas, and urban health facilities will produce higher population growth rates for city people and, thus, for the country as a whole.[38]

Crime control is already emerging as another first-order crisis.

[36] Ruth First, *Power in Africa*, New York: Random House, 1970, p. 359.
[37] Free, *The Attitudes, Hopes and Fears of Nigerians*, pp. 46–47.
[38] Akin L. Mabogunje, *Urbanization in Nigeria*, New York: Africana Publishing Co., 1968, p. 315. Mabogunje's book includes case studies of Ibadan and Lagos.

The peak in political crime, with 158 election-connected murders in 1964–1965, has given way in the postwar era to armed robbery.[39] An indication of one approach to be taken toward the crime problem was given by the public execution of four convicted armed robbers in Warri on March 20, 1971. Twenty thousand spectators witnessed the execution held in the midwestern city's sports arena.

Crime, unemployment, and expensive and unproductive military establishment, strikes, and urban blight are samples of dilemmas the military government will have to face in order to meet the anticipated growth rate. Successful development will require more than good technical coordination, and adequate capital. Intangibles, principally the lack of the peoples' will to sacrifice, from high levels to low, were unforeseen factors in the First Development Plan that have to be reckoned with. When that plan was first underway, one economist reported that he could not find "a single Nigerian who was not critical. People who greeted the plan with high hopes are now discouraged." [40] This malaise did not escape those who have forged the Second Plan. According to the new Plan, "One major difficulty in the [first] plan's administration was that, except in some government circles, the average Nigerian did not identify himself with the plan . . . previous plans did not adequately reflect the aspirations of the country."[41] How the leadership approaches these interlocking questions of communications, motivation, and policy is, of course, crucial. Nigeria's planners have begun to come to grips with the human factors in development, and that is a good sign.

[39] Crime statistics are given in T. N. Tamuno, The Police in Modern Nigeria, Ibadan: Oxford University Press, 1971.
[40] Sayre P. Schatz, "Nigeria's First National Development Plan (1962–1968) An Appraisal," Nigerian Institute of Social and Economic Research, Reprint Series, no. 3 (1963):221.
[41] Second National Development Plan, 1970–1974, p. 16.

CHAPTER NINE

Foreign Policy

As WITH DOMESTIC POLICY, Nigeria's foreign policies since the conclusion of the civil war have changed considerably from those of
the First Republic. Militantly nationalistic views held by the
bureaucrat-army leadership have combined with events since 1966
to produce an outlook which is at once more defensive and
suspicious in relations with the world and its power struggles, and
more assertive within its own West African region. This survey
of Nigerian foreign policy will begin with some comments on the
process of foreign policy making. Then the chapter will review
the First Republic's surprisingly good record, and the largely
deleterious impact of the civil war on her relations with Africa
and much of the world, and the procedures and directions of
foreign policy for the 1970s.

The Making of Foreign Policy

It is popular among political scientists to talk of the widening
disparity between foreign policy making in new, as opposed to
established, states. One can easily draw an analogy between planning in the domestic and in the international arenas. Nigerian
foreign policy planners know less than their American counterparts about the conditions to which they may have to respond,
just as domestic development planners find themselves constrained
by inadequate knowledge of their own economy's performance.

This situation for example, limits the everyday operation of Nigerian immigration and visitation policy, as the number of trained personnel capable of handling passport and visa functions is too limited for the sometimes overambitious plans. During 1971, for example, Nigerian embassies were directed to refer all passport and visa applications to the Lagos Ministry of External Affairs for a ruling. Delays in handling the applications lasted weeks, then months. By July 1971, this tactic was so unmanageable that embassies were directed to issue visas of up to three months without referring back to Lagos. The irony of this situation is that despite fewer trained individuals, Nigeria seemed determined to operate a visitations policy which requires impressive screening capacities. Chief Anthony Enahoro, a Yoruba politician jailed during the treason trials and subsequently released, commented perceptively on this dilemma in 1965, and the situation had not improved by 1971.

We must liberalize our immigration regulations and procedure, open our doors and let daylight into our country. Nigerians take kindly to strangers. The stringent restrictions to which intending visitors and businessmen, even from Commonwealth countries, are subject do not derive from the national character. Nigerian officialdom tends to treat prospective visitors to Nigeria as suspicious characters on the assumption that the world is constantly seeking to subvert our state. This is ridiculous. . . . What have we to hide?[1]

If everyday foreign relations functions are adversely affected by this combination of inadequate machinery and expansive aims, the research and policy-making functions of Nigerian diplomacy also suffer. Again ironically, policies which are designed increasingly to show Nigeria's independence from any outside interference and neocolonialism are frequently made on the basis of information derived from those very outside sources.[2]

[1] Chief Anthony Enahoro, *Fugitive Offender: The Story of a Political Prisoner*, London: Cassell, 1965, p. 395.
[2] David M. Gray, "The Foreign Policy Process in the Emerging African Nation: Nigeria and Ghana," Philadelphia: University of Pennsylvania, *Studies of Social Values and Public Policy* (January, 1962), Memo #2.

Foreign Policy 1960–1970

During the terminal colonial period, Nigerian leaders were quite naturally preoccupied with the problems of self-government, and comparatively little effort was expended on foreign policy.[3] By 1960, such evidence as exists indicates that a widespread consensus prevailed on most major foreign policy issues. The leadership of all three major political parties was decidedly pro-Western by virtue of educational background, ideology, and political contacts. Asked whether their country should side with the West or Communist world, Nigerian legislators answered in favor of siding with Britain and the United States, 41 percent, with the U.S.S.R., 2 percent.[4] Britain's generous outlook toward Nigerian independence offered little encouragement to advocates of a vigorous breakaway from Western influence. Most of the significant political elite anticipated Commonwealth membership and continued close relations with Britain. Nonetheless, the new Nigeria subscribed to the popular Afro-Asian concept on "nonalignment." Free notes further that 57 percent of the First Federal Legislature favored staying out of cold war entanglements, as opposed to 36 percent who favored clearly choosing sides. As the Federal Prime Minister explained to the United Nations, nonalignment did not necessarily mean "neutrality," but rather the absence of routine alignment with either cold war camp.[5]

The Nigerians interpreted nonalignment as a pragmatic policy which would allow decisions to be made on the merits of issues while maintaining flexibility. To stress the positive nature of this policy, which many Americans have equated with support for

[3] This preoccupation seems to have continued after independence, as indicated in interview data by Lloyd Free, who noted in 1962 that their lack of concern about international war or peace was "about the most marked we have recorded to date." *The Attitudes, Hopes and Fears of Nigerians*, p. 53.

[4] *Ibid.*, p. 5.

[5] For reviews of foreign policy during Nigeria's first independent years, see Ezera, *Constitutional Developments*, pp. 292 ff. John P. Mackintosh, "Nigerian External Relations," in Mackintosh, ed. *Nigerian Government*, and Claude S. Phillips, Jr., *The Development of Nigerian Foreign Policy*, Evanston, Ill.: Northwestern University Press, 1964.

our enemies, Nigerians embellished their intentions with reference to the impact of the emerging "African personality." on world politics. The presence of many new African states after 1960 would result, the argument went, in a beneficial, stabilizing influence on existing world tensions. Africans were not simply "little Frenchmen" or "little Englishmen," and their distinct approach to life would have a double impact on the world stage. The 'African identity' would finally be obvious to all, and world tensions would feel the Africans' moderating influence.

Nonalignment is in many ways a natural consequence of the colonial relationship. Nigerians of north and south may have differed in approach toward internal political, economic, or social issues, but virtually all felt some degree of hostility towards any hint of condescension by their former colonial master. Other white nations were similarly suspect, and not the least of these by any means was the United States. Though officially anticolonialist, America was closely allied with the former colonial powers and was rich and enviable in the bargain. To disassociate themselves from the world that held them in colonial subjection, Nigerians frequently identified with political and social ideals that stressed their distinctiveness, such as "African socialism" and "African personality." This phenomenon emerged at many different levels, notably in criticism of Western "hypocrisy" by Nigerian intellectuals. The Ijaw poet, J. P. Clark, who has traveled and studied in the United States, commented:

> The old credo of the right of private property and of the inherent ability and right of man to exploit an existing opportunity for wealth sounds as good as ever in the American ear. It matters little that with the collapse of the frontier the chief articles in the Creed have also lost all their foundations.[6]

Even in comparison with their own recent experience, many Nigerians see the United States as a materialistic and violent society.[7] Vitriolic reactions greet any apparent condescension and

[6] John Pepper Clark, America, Their America, New York: Africana, 1969, p. 129.

[7] For example, the views of a Nigerian student as reported in The New York Times, December 9, 1970. Travel to the United States seems to intensify anti-American views, See Clark, America and Free, The Attitudes, Hopes and Fears of Nigerians, p. 21.

pity from Americans who are depressed by living conditions in Nigeria. During the Kennedy era, a Peace Corps girl left Nigeria after a public furor about a postcard home in which she had depicted Ibadan's "primitive" conditions. In A Man of the People, Chinua Achebe describes this emotion well through Odili's anger at his white American guest's criticism of Lagos' slums: "I began to wonder whether Jean actually enjoyed driving through these places as she claimed she did or whether she had some secret reason, like wanting me to feel ashamed about my country's capital city." [8]

"Ambivalent" perhaps best describes the psychological bases of Nigeria's early foreign policy. Deeply distrustful and suspicious of any new form of postcolonial subjection, Nigerians also envied and wished to emulate Western achievement. Anxious not to be associated with capitalism, imperialism, and class-structured society, many advocated a distinct approach to economics and politics. However, as products of Western influence through education and missionary activity, most Nigerian elite found it impossible to subscribe to political and economic theories which were totally at odds with the West.

From the outset, Nigeria's foreign policy decisions were by necessity compromises between ties with Britain and other Western countries, prompted by the need for procuring aid, and the desire to establish a "Nigerian" identity. These concerns were obviously contradictory, and provided the main basis for attacks on the Balewa Government during 1960–1962. As leader of the federal opposition, Awolowo employed criticism of foreign policy directions as a major tactic, until he was stripped of political power in 1962. A firm pro-Westerner during the colonial era, once he was in a position to assail the federal government's apparent postindependence alignment with the Western countries, Awolowo became an advocate of vigorous nonalignment. [9]

In early 1960, two years after a defense agreement had been signed as part of the constitutional negotiations between the British Colonial Office and Nigerian politicians, a heated debate

---

[8] Achebe, A Man of the People, p. 51.

[9] On Awolowo's foreign policy views, see Ezera, Constitutional Developments, p. 293.

over the provisions of the treaty began. Awolowo charged that Nigerian participants in the London Conference had been forced to sign the defense pact or face delays in the independence timetable. By February 1960, independence was still nine months away, and Balewa had just assumed responsibility for defense policies. It was then that time had come to demonstrate the vigor of the opposition. The defense pact, kept secret until February 1960, provided the substance for argument. Awolowo and other critics attacked provisions for transit rights and for tropical training facilities for British forces. In reality, it was the symbolic nature of the pact that was most objectionable to the Nigerian critics.[10] Revised in mid-1960, the pact was finally abrogated in January 1962.

The vigorous opposition offered by the AG to the issue of the defense pact with Britain should not cloud the relative unity of foreign policy in the First Republic, at least when compared to the disastrous divisions over internal politics. Table 10 shows the comparative unity shown by the three main parliamentary parties in the First Federal Legislature on the question of entangling international alliances.

One probable cause of these shared viewpoints can be found in the psychological effects of colonialism. All history-conscious

Table 10.   Legislative Attitudes Toward International Alliances

| Legislators who felt Nigeria | Political Party | | |
should side with	NPC	NCNC	AG
U.S.A., UK, etc.	51%	21%	30%
U.S.S.R., etc.	—	4%	—
Neither bloc	49%	54%	50%
Qualified answers	—	21%	10%
No opinion	—	—	10%

Source: Lloyd A. Free, *The Attitudes, Hopes and Fears of Nigerians,* Princeton, N.J.; Institute for International and Social Research, 1964, p. 6.

[10] A detailed description of the defense pact is found in Gordon J. Idang, "The Politics of Nigerian Foreign Policy: The Ratification and Renunciation of the Anglo-Nigerian Defense Agreement," *African Studies Review* XIII, no. 2 (September, 1970): 227–252.

Nigerians, whether Moslem, Christian, or pagan, whether Ibo or Hausa, shared deep feelings of race consciousness, which produced a unanimity of opinion on many foreign issues. Nigeria condemned France for Saharan atomic tests, blasted South Africa and Portugal for their continued political repression of blacks, and declined associate status in the European Common Market in spite of the obvious economic advantages such cooperation would have offered for the sale of Nigerian commodities. In matters which found Nigeria in contact with non-African governments, a degree of unity prevailed which made the argument over the defense pact something of an exception.

This unity was more tenuous when it came to intra-African matters. Like most other African countries, Nigeria gained independence 3 years after Ghana, a lag which allowed the Ghanaian President, Kwame Nkrumah, to establish his voice as predominant among pan-Africanists. Nkrumah's espoused policy for all of Africa was to "seek first the political kingdom," which implied the forging of federal unity through creation of a strong pan-African organization. But as the new African states emerged, their leaders were quickly caught up in the issues of self-government, and gave little thought to pan-Africanism. Most saw Nkrumah's initiative as a threat to their own national sovereignty, although some African nations (Mali, Guinea) did embrace Nkrumah's theories and attempted to create federal unions with Ghana.

Nigeria was among the majority to resist this trend, but not without internal opposition. Awolowo was typical of those who objected to Nigeria's conservatism in African affairs. Many of the more "radical African nationalist" elements in Nigeria disliked the prospect of Ghana in the vanguard of African consciousness while the "giant of Africa" appeared to slumber. They therefore resisted their government's support of the United Nations force and the Kasavubu regime during the Congo crisis. The Awolowo group championed Lumumba and his memory. By 1962, the net effect of these initiatives by critics of the Balewa government's policies was to stimulate a more active role for Nigeria. Nigerian leaders served as the major moderators in the discussion that led to the Organization of African Unity (OAU) in 1963. Nigeria's subsequent role in inter-African relations will be treated later in this chapter.

In view of the disruptive internal politics of the First Republic and varying depths of actual racial animosity which Nigerian leaders had experienced (Azikiwe was subjected to more prejudice in his expatriate days as a doctor in the white Western world than Balewa), the degree of positive impact made by Nigerian foreign policy up to 1966 was surprising. However, there was no drastic reversal of ties with the West. Economic development during the colonial era had shaped an overwhelming pro-Western bias that no amount of political intentions could rapidly overcome. Youth and student organizations and the official Action Group opposition put forth a continual blast of criticisms against government failure to be purely nonaligned, and these critics were far from pleased with the results.

Actually, the First Republic government did attempt to establish economic relations with Communist countries. Trade missions and agreements were sought with China, Russia, and several East European nations between June 1961, and July 1963. While the total proportion of trade with these countries was not impressive until recently, these initiatives did involve the Nigerians in some delicate negotiations with the United States, which under the Battle Act of 1951 (named for Congressman Lucius Battle) forbade American aid to any nation which "Knowingly permits the shipment [of primary strategic items] to any nation or combination of nations threatening the security of the United States, including the Union of Soviet Socialist Republics and all countries under its domination. . . ." [11] The drop in demand for columbite, a strategic material used as a steel additive, caused a difficult situation after 1956. The United States had stockpiled large amounts of columbite and Nigeria, with much of the world's supply, now wished to sell it elsewhere. By the 1960s, America had come to view trade with communist states by its allies and aid recipients with less hostility than during the McCarthy era. Knowing this, the Nigerians ignored mild American warnings and

[11] Douglas Anglin, "Nigeria: Political Non-alignment and Economic Alignment," *Journal of Modern African Studies* 3, no. 2 (July, 1964):251.

offered columbite to the U.S.S.R. As one student of the First Republic's foreign policy has concluded: "If the issue did come to a showdown, there is little doubt that Nigerians would willingly, if perhaps unwisely, forgo American aid rather than accept an infringement of their sovereignty."[12] That same scholar concluded that on balance Nigeria's early foreign policy generally failed to be predictably pro-Western in accordance with aid and trade ties. Pro-Western positions, such as not visiting Cuba, not recognizing the East German regime of Walther Ulbricht, and remaining a member of the Commonwealth, were more than balanced by decisions which ran counter to Nigeria's Western-oriented economic ties: offering columbite to Russia, trade agreements with communist countries, rejecting associate Common Market status, abrogating the defense pact, condemning France's Saharan nuclear tests, and vigorously criticizing South Africa. On balance, from an African perspective the First Republic's foreign policy could certainly not be accused of slavish pro-Westernism.

Effects of the Biafran War on Nigerian Foreign Policy

Three years of civil war have seriously affected Nigerian contacts with the rest of the world. Overwhelming Western influence has been eroded, in exchange for a considerable increase in Soviet presence. Table 11 shows the dramatic rise in Soviet-Nigerian trade. By 1968, the volume of Nigeria's trade with the U.S.S.R. placed her fourth among African countries, behind U.A.R., Algeria, and Morocco.[13] With the civil war concluded, the valuable military aid received from Soviet Russia has been replaced by new agreements. Nigerian recognition of Communist China is a further indication of the new spirit of initiative the Nigerians now feel.

With its heavily Western orientation, Nigeria's economy will in all likelihood retain significant trade ties with Britain and

[12] Ibid., p. 253.
[13] G. Rubenstein, "Aspects of Soviet-African Economic Relations," Journal of Modern African Studies 8, no. 3 (October, 1970):390.

Table 11. Nigeria's Foreign Trade, 1960–1970 (in millions of U.S. dollars)

	1960	1966	1967	1968	1969	1970 (1st 7 mo.)
Exports to:						
1. United States	45	63	53	49	112	71
2. United Kingdom	226	295	199	174	246	211
3. Netherlands	60	73	87	76	120	111
4. Germany (Fed. Rep.)	36	78	71	50	54	45
5. Communist bloc	2	9	21	28	29	25
Imports from:						
1. United States	32	116	78	62	82	77
2. United Kingdom	256	214	181	168	242	179
3. Japan	78	40	53	20	26	33
4. Germany (Fed. Rep.)	43	77	71	59	74	50
5. Communist bloc	11	27	38	33	38	28
Totals:						
Exports	475	793	587	905	1,235 (est.)	
Imports	−604	−718	−541	−696	−1,100 (est.)	
Trade balance	−129	75	46	209	135	

Source: U.S.A.I.D., Economic Data Book, Africa. Revision No. 257, April 1971, p. 6.

America. There is no doubt, however, that Nigerian leaders felt betrayed in their darkest hour by those nations, and have tried since 1970 to identify and develop new sources of trade and aid. The Japanese, for example, have extended a loan worth $24 million and are now the fourth largest exporter of goods to Nigeria, after Britain, America, and West Germany. Nigeria's early 1971 recognition of Communist China, a country that has begun to reassert its presence in Africa after a period of discredit caused by mid-1960 political intrigues and by the internal turmoils of her Cultural Revolution, is further evidence of this trend. According to Nigeria's Minister of External Affairs, Dr. Okoi Arikpo, the decision to recognize the mainland government of China reflects a postwar desire to "build a truly Nigerian society." [14]

Recent Nigerian relations with Britain have reflected the division within Britain as to what constitutes wise policy toward a Nigeria divided by civil war. The British have long been committed to the idea of a strong, united Nigeria, and during the early 1960s were more willing than Awolowo and other southerners to accept growing northern hegemony over the federation. Indeed, the turnover of British governments up to June 1970 seemed to assure British accommodation to political developments in Nigeria. Dominance by the Hausa-Fulani was certainly less noxious to British Conservative Government than to Wilson's Labour cabinet, which took power in October 1964. Subsequently, the Labour party was more inclined to support the concept of a unified Nigeria under the postcoup, minority-influenced government, as long as its nondemocratic structure was considered temporary. During the civil war, British government support of the Federal side was constant albeit materially insufficient from the Nigerian point of view. The tensions in British–Nigerian relations must be attributed to reaction by the British public; from 1968 on, the tide of public opinion turned away from supporting the Federal case, a change prompted mostly by concern for the welfare and survival of the Ibo people. Particularly during the

[14] Extensive reports of Nigeria's new foreign policy directions appeared in *Le Monde*, December 2, 1970, and *The New York Times*, April 9, 1971.

last year of the war, reports of starvation in Biafra, shrinking and encircled, resulted in sometimes harsh parliamentary debate, in which the Wilson government was accused of covering up "the facts" in their pursuit of an apparently bankrupt policy. It was quite possible for even the well-informed Englishman to believe, right up to the last month of the war, that Biafran "will," devotion to Ojukwu, and discipline, would more than compensate for Nigerian numbers and firepower. The civil war had demonstrated many cases of weak government command over federal units, and of "final offensives" that had become Federal fiascos. Thus, during 1968 and 1969, many Britains, Americans, and other outsiders fully expected the conflict to end in negotiations, and in a virtually independent Biafran state. France (with her close African ally, Ivory Coast, one of the four African states to recognize Biafra) was clearly counting on this development, and encouraged Biafra. De Gaulle and his foreign affairs expert on Africa, Jacques Foccart, seemed to be viewing independent Africa in terms of the nineteenth century, when England presented the greatest challenge to France.

While France had clearly chosen to sacrifice relations with the Nigerian Federal Government, Britain appeared as an ally who could not be trusted, in spite of the protestations of support from government civil servants in London, and officials stationed in Lagos.[15] The unexpectedly quick Federal victory in January 1970, and the improvement throughout that year of the initially grim medical situation in Iboland, might have been cited by Wilson's government as proof of their case that the Federal Nigerian side had deserved Britain's support all along. The clamor over Nigeria's affairs by British Parliamentarians, journalists, and the public might have been forgotten, if in June 1970, the conservative Heath Cabinet had not unexpectedly defeated the Labour party, putting into power those very Tory critics of the Labour government who had called for a hands-off policy that would have aided the Ibo secession. Naturally, Nigerian-British relations were bound to cool off.

15 In a heavily pro-Biafran account, Frederic Forsyth provides some interesting insights into the influence of British policy. The Biafran Story, Baltimore: Penguin, 1969, ch. 10.

If Britain joins the European Common Market without some-how compensating for Nigeria's loss of Commonwealth markets for cocoa, relations may deteriorate even further. The Nigerian at-titude toward Commonwealth affiliation is changing inexorably in any case as "Let's leave the Commonwealth," a 1971 editorial in New Nigerian, testifies.

> For those member countries that are not inhabited by people of British descent, the Commonwealth is no more than an imperial junk yard bordered by strong, almost invisible, silken threads from which it will take much more than the normal political courage and will power left in the breasts of the mentally emasculated and suitably educationally conditioned mind of the ex-colonial man to escape. . . . It is only by deliberately deciding to leave the Commonwealth can we begin to recreate the political elan with which to move forward under our own steam.[16]

Current Nigerian–American relations suffer from a similar set of circumstances, though the timing of events differs. The princi-pal difficulty is that Nigeria (and Africa generally) is deemed so relatively inconsequential to American foreign relations, while to Britain, Africa has always been of major importance. Probably because of this, America has tended to defer to British initiatives. Our view of Nigeria in the early 1960s as a model for African democracy followed the British lead, though perhaps for different reasons: Britain's trade interests were more weighty and her con-cern for supporting the existing regime as a road to stability was more vested than ours.

Our early "Nigeriaphilia" continued to have strong supporters in high places during the Johnson years. Our first ambassador to Nigeria, Joseph Palmer, then served Johnson (and Nixon briefly) as Under Secretary of State in charge of African Affairs. Our diplomats and foreign policy makers had little difficulty accepting Britain's view on the eve of the confrontation, that we should support the Federal side in hopes that the expected quick victory could "keep Nigeria one," and be less painful in terms of human suffering. While, in the midst of our Vietnam commitments, we

[16] New Nigerian, January 8, 1971, p. 1.

could offer no arms or material aid in putting down Biafra, we assured the Federal side that we sympathized with their cause.

As 1968 unfolded, the Gowon government began to realize that American support, like that of the British, was not to be trusted unequivocally. Biafran public relations and propaganda began to make their mark on American minds, and people who were perhaps too hungry for humanitarian causes at that particular moment began to react against the prospects of "genocide." American emotions were touched by a vision of the unfortunate Ibo, portrayed as usual in terms that made them seem the very epitome of American values, being blasted by turbanned Federal Moslems in their Russian MIGs. The "new left" made Biafra a campaign issue and in 1968–1969, Senator Eugene McCarthy and New York's Paul O'Dwyer were among those who blasted Johnson's government for doing nothing while Biafra starved. Candidate Richard Nixon also saw the political potential of the Biafran issue. Nixon gave what was probably his most eloquent campaign speech on the importance of Biafran relief, which he viewed as "thwarted by the desire of the central government of Nigeria to pursue total and unconditional victory." In his criticism of the Johnson government's hesitancy, he continued:

[G]enocide is what is taking place right now—and starvation is the grim reaper. This is not the time to stand on ceremony, or to "go through channels" or to observe the diplomatic niceties. The destruction of an entire people is an immoral objective even in the most moral of wars. It can never be justified; it can never be condoned.[17]

Amid mounting stories of atrocities against the Ibo, Nixon took power in January 1969. It is easy to imagine the misgivings on the Nigerian side. Sure of the justness of their cause, Nigerians must have considered increased Russian aid an obvious solution. At least Soviet leadership could be counted on to remain in power and survive the whims of public opinion, whatever their ultimate aims!

Though Nigeria's Federal Government had cause to suspect continued official American assurances of support, Washington

---

[17] Forsyth, *The Biafra Story*, p. 163.

did not really carry out any acts of aid for the Biafran secessionists. In fact, though Nixon apparently wished to do something about Biafra relief, the State Department may have actively frustrated Administration attempts, suspecting that any such actions would prolong the war and lose the friendship of the Nigerian government.[18] In the long run, and with the benefit of hindsight, this seemed quite sensible. State Department "regulars" intended to be sure that no president could wreck United States–Nigerian relations for the sake of political gains he might reap by saving a few starving Ibos. Hence, some critics have maintained that the diplomats and foreign policy strategists intentionally "dragged their feet" rather than spur relief initiatives that were sure to offend the Gowon government.[19]

Particularly harmful to United States–Nigerian relations were two events that occurred immediately following the Biafran war. The Internal Revenue Service designated the Nigerian War Victims Relief Foundation (based in New York City) as a tax exempt organization, an action that appeared to the Federal Nigerian Government as official American support for Biafra. Nigeria protested that these types of organizations were not primarily involved with relief efforts, but were collecting support for a Biafran Government-in-exile. In Washington, Nigeria's Ambassador, Joseph Iyalla declared: "Nigeria would not accept their assistance or support in any form or manner, since [these Ibo] were regarded as having the blood of many Nigerians on their hands." [20]

These annoyances followed a tense situation during the first days after Biafra's surrender. Americans were becoming increasingly alarmed by reports of Biafra's "starving millions." The Nigerian Government played down such reports, claiming the ability to handle internal problems adequately without foreign help. President Nixon's strategy was to inform the Nigerians im-

[18] Two interesting articles make this argument in *Ripon Forum*, February, 1969, pp. 5–11, and March, 1970, pp. 8–19.

[19] Some of the criticisms of the *Ripon Forum* articles are countered by the Under Secretary of State, Elliot L. Richardson, in *Ripon Forum*, March, 1970, p. 28.

[20] *The New York Times*, September 27, 1970.

mediately of the seriousness of Ibo malnutrition; an extensive report by Dr. Karl Western of United States Public Health Service, carried out in Biafra, confirmed the gloomiest predictions. State Department officials in Washington and Lagos delayed in presenting the report, assuming correctly that the Nigerians would dislike being told by other governments about conditions in their own country! By the time pressure from President Nixon's office resulted in the disclosure to Gowon's government of Dr. Western's information, the Nigerians' position had hardened against the necessity of massive outside aid.[21] The Nigerians perferred to believe the report of Lord Hunt's mission, which concluded that the press had overreported the famine. Hunt's view was that Nigeria's own relief effort was hurt by "this phenomenon of human caring, skillfully exploited for political ends . . ." which had magnified "the scale and nature of the problem to an astonishing degree."[22] Thus American policy achieved the dual disaster of having no impact on the relief situation and alienating the Federal Government! The Nigerians' outspoken revulsion in United Nations debate to America's decision of late 1971 to purchase Rhodesian chrome confirms the cumulative impact of these events.

To summarize, one major result of Nigeria's recent relations with the world powers has been a net decrease in cordial relations with Britain, America, and France. The Nigerians will have to be reassured by events of this decade that the Western countries do not intend to interfere in Nigeria's affairs, and favorable conditions do seem to exist. In fact, changes within the Western countries themselves (Britain's argument over the Common Market and European unity, America's comparative isolationism resulting from Vietnam) may soon have Nigeria and other African countries worried about the effects of the opposite condition—"that the outside world generally . . . are less interested

[21] *Ripon Forum*, March, 1970, p. 11. Again, see Richardson's defense against these charges.
[22] United Kingdom Government, "Nigeria: The Problem of Relief in the Aftermath of the Nigerian Civil War: Report of Lord Hunt's Mission," *Command Paper #4275*, January, 1970, p. 4.

in tropical Africa than they were, or than Africans had supposed."[23] Whether this decline in Africa's importance in the minds of out- siders will operate to Africa's advantage or disadvantage remains to be seen.

The second significant shift in Nigeria's foreign contacts is its new relationship with the U.S.S.R. A decade ago, a close observer of Nigerian attitudes noted the Nigerian leadership's ability to subordinate their opposition to racial discrimination in America to their desires for continued American "helpfulness."[24] Likewise we can probably expect Nigeria's leaders to be as tolerant now of the Soviet Union's internal deficiencies in view of the recent substantial aid given by the Russians.

Nigeria and African Affairs

The best record achieved by the ill-fated First Republic was undoubtedly in the area of continental affairs. Although refusing to assume a neutral stance, Nigeria was the voice of moderation and her spokesmen were effective mediators between contending views of African organization.

Present indications are that Nigeria's role in African affairs will be more assertive than during the First Republic. For example, twice since the Biafran war concluded, Nigeria has offered the use of her troops to other African states—to Guinea in November 1970, during the period of "invasions" from Portuguese Guinea, and to Chad during the same year for use in quelling the rebellion in that neighbor's northern desert areas. The December 1970 Lagos Conference on the Guinean question gave Nigeria new diplomatic prestige. With its well-equipped military of over 200,000 men Nigeria is now obviously the "giant of Africa" in a new sense. This section will survey Nigeria's African concerns from two per- spectives—as a part of the international relations of the entire continent, and as the dominant power in the West African region.

Nigeria's role in Africa has been to organize African continental

---

[23] Scipio, Emergent Africa, New York: Simon & Schuster, 1965, p. 121.
[24] Free, The Attitudes, Hopes and Fears of Nigerians, pp. 12–15.

cooperation on specific issues. Toward the same end, Nkrumah, Ghana's President, favored different tactics, the merger of sovereignties at the top, or "federalism" as a step toward the expansion of a larger and more formidable political union. In his view, defending Africa's hard-won freedom would necessitate a unity which the continent's colonial balkanization prevented. He saw no alternative but to pool resources in areas of economic planning, transportation and communications, and defense. The centralizing of executive power would be required to achieve this goal. However, he was never successful in convincing other new heads of state that his envisioned "United States of Africa" was not merely a vehicle for his own ambitions.

Nkrumah's first attempts met with some success. In 1958, Guineans rebuked De Gaulle's offer of a new postcolonial relationship with France by voting against the Fifth Republic Constitution. Vindictively cut off by the French, Sékou Touré welcomed association with Ghana. The declaration passed by the two countries, meeting in Conakry in May 1959, offered the Guinea-Ghana Union as the first step toward a "union" of African states. The vast majority of today's new African states were, at that time, still preparing for independence, but Liberia had been acknowledged as a sovereign state for over a century. Her president, William V. S. Tubman, reacted against the Ghana-Guinea Union, stressing in a July 1959, meeting with Touré and Nkrumah that the "community" of African states, as he preferred to call it, could achieve its objective without jeopardizing the national identity of its constitutent states.

Nigeria was to become perhaps the most significant arbiter in this emerging dabate, at the Second Conference of Independent African States in June 1960. After the Ghanaian Foreign Minister stressed the Nkrumahist concept of political union, the Nigerian delegate crystallized the objections of many new countries who were participating in pan-African discussions for the first time as independent states.

> Pan Africanism is the only solution to our problems in Africa. . . . But we must not be sentimental . . . the idea of forming a Union of African States is premature . . . it is essential to remember that what-

ever ideas we may have about pan-Africanism it will not materialize, or at least it will not materialize as quickly as we would like it to if we start building from the top downwards. We must first prepare the minds of the different African countries—we must start from the known to the unknown. At the moment, we in Nigeria cannot afford to form union by government with any African States by surrendering our sovereignty.[25]

The Nigerians were offering a more modest approach to continental unity—the gradual cementing of functional cooperation in specific policy areas, or "functionalism." Against their view, the Nkrumahist "federalists" argued that political union, from the top downwards could "provide the framework within which any plans for economic, social and cultural co-operation" could be carried out.

To a large extent, Nkrumahist-style boldness in advocating pan-Africanism through political union coincide with several other related issues on more local levels. Ghana's support came principally from states who faced specific losses if they condoned loose, confederal political solutions. A group of twelve former French colonies met in October 1960, at Brazzaville, advocating just such a functional emphasis toward pan-African cooperation. This group favored recognition of the confederalist Congo regime that had ousted Lumumba, and acknowledgement of Mauretania's claimed individuality from Morocco. In January 1960, Ghana and her cohorts met at Casablanca to reassert their opposing views: Morocco claimed parts of Mauretania, and the Arab states called for pan-African unity against Israel. Ghana, Guinea, and Mali exchanged their support on these issues for North African backing of their refusal to acknowledge Lumumba's successors.

In May 1961, the cleavage between two groups of African states was completed when Nigeria and six others joined the twelve "Brazzaville moderates" to demonstrate that Africa's majority refused to fall in behind Nkrumah. A period of intense bitterness followed, with Ghana and Nigeria, the chief protagonists, waging a battle of words. The fundamental difference be-

[25] Colin Legum, *Pan-Africanism*, New York: Praeger, 1962, pp. 46–47.

tween Nkrumahism and the Nigerian position was supported to
some extent by the Nigerian Federal opposition. Though they
criticized the Balewa government for failing to capture the initiative in African continental politics, Awolowo and his cohorts
advocated a confederal form of African cooperation which would
have fallen short of Nkrumah's intentions to "unify" Africa.[26]

Just when independent Africa seemed (excluding the white
minority regimes of southern Africa) fundamentally and irretrieva-
bly split into two camps, Nigeria had her finest hour in foreign
policy. Through persistent diplomacy, the Balewa government
led the contestants to the discussion table once again, and the
Organization of African Unity was formed. The 1963 Charter of
the OAU left no doubt that major points of Nkrumah's policy
had been defeated; there were specific warnings, for example,
against meddling in the internal affairs of Africa's "sovereign
states." However, the Charter did retain a tone of militancy,
particularly toward continued white control in southern Africa,
to appease the more radical states, and the OAU was joined by
the full memberships of the Brazzaville and Casablanca groups.

The OAU's formation does not justify the belief that the continent's divisive issues had suddenly melted away. Even in the
victory of moderate approaches toward cooperation, functional
commissions had been created to work on continental problems,
and the OAU and some of its specific commissions had become
involved in political issues facing the African states. Nigeria's
response to political aspects of the OAU's work falls into three
stages. Until 1967, through her position as one of nine member
states on the OAU's Liberation Commission, Nigeria supported
the OAU policy of opposition to continued Portuguese and
Afrikaner control over Black Africans. She also supported OAU
mediations of several border conflicts. However, when the OAU
Council of Ministers requested all member states to break diplomatic relations with Britain to protest Rhodesia's successful
unilateral declaration of independence, Balewa was outspoken in
insisting that only a full meeting of the OAU Legislative As-

26 *Ibid.*, p. 58.

sembly (with all states represented) could make such a binding decision.[27]

During the civil war, Nigeria became the subject of OAU efforts. At first, the OAU initiatives were thwarted by Nigeria's view that the revolt was an internal matter, and that only the total surrender of the "criminal" Ojukwu would suffice. Then as the number of casualties increased, as Biafran resistance became more fabled, and as non-African powers competed for the favor of one side or the other, the OAU was rent by the same argument that was internally dividing Britain and the United States. Should the Ibo be forced by the threat of annihilation to remain members of a system in which they had lost faith? One of the most respected "radical" African leaders, Julius Nyerere of Tanzania, recognized Biafra, apparently hoping that the Gowon regime could be helped to accept the reality of Biafra if other African countries exerted pressure. The Ivory Coast, respected among French-speaking moderate states, did the same. By the end of the conflict only two other African countries, Gabon and Zambia, had recognized Biafra, but the fact remains that Nigeria's civil war brought about an unexpected continental reaction; serious questioning of the concept of One Nigeria, even from countries that contain their own potential Biafras. We cannot be certain yet what impact this mixture of reactions among African states will have on Nigerian faith in the OAU, but it would not be surprising if Nigeria operates more in accord with her own specific interests in the future.

On the part of Nigeria the postwar period has been a time of renewed interest in African affairs. General Gowon has traveled to many African countries, but rarely outside the continent. In November 1971, Gowon and three other African heads of state went to Israel and Egypt to promote solutions to an enduring crisis that diverts Arab attentions and resources from African problems. Another significant visit was Gowon's April 1971 trip to Senegal. The Nigerian leadership now seems concerned with its role in raising African consciousness by promoting such con-

[27] John Markakis, "The O.A.U.: A Progress Report," *Journal of Modern African Studies* 4, no. 2 (October, 1966):146.

cepts as "negritude" and "African personality." Planning has begun for the second world festival of black arts and culture to be held near Lagos in 1974. Nigeria plans to spend $25 million on this event, which follows up the 1966 festival in Senegal. Possibly related to this trend is the decline of Wole Soyinka, the Nigerian playwright who has condemned the idea of negritude, and the rise of new faces like the University of Ife's Abiola Irele, a firm advocate of the concept. Other evidence of this awakening is the new Franz Fanon Research Center in Enugu, directed by Chinua Achebe, which has been charged with a "total commitment to the mental emancipation of the black men all over the world from neo-colonial mentality." [28] This cultural militancy supplements Nigeria's distinctly militant stance in recent continental political affairs. At the June 1971 OAU Summit Conference, Gowon argued for a 3-year timetable of action that would result in the freeing of at least one remaining colonial territory.

Nigeria's earlier reluctance to support grand schemes for swift African unity may be entirely reversed during the 1970s. Nigerian military leaders were even discussing the feasibility of an African joint high command structure that would allow more effective coordination of the various national armies for defense against such attacks as occurred in Guinea in November 1970. The Federal Military Government may also be planning to do something concrete about the claim that OAU should liberate at least one colonial territory during the next 3 years. Amilcar Cabral, the leader of the Portuguese Guinea liberation movement, was an unflinching supporter of the Federal side during Nigeria's civil war. His movement would probably be the most likely recipient of help from any "High Command" the Nigerians could succeed in setting up.

There are other Nigerians, particularly among the civil service elite, who are likely to question these military initiatives. Men like Foreign Minister Okoi Arikpo are more conscious of the sensibilities of smaller African states, and will probably restrain the officers. Given the size of Nigeria's armed forces, and the

[28] *West Africa*, December 26, 1970 and January 1, 1971, p. 1522.

ability of subordinate officers to spend money needlessly, ways to put their postwar strength to "legitimate" use are obviously welcome to the military high command.

Nigeria and her Neighbors

Dahomey, Niger, Chad, Cameroon, and Equatorial Guinea have had few complaints about their relations with Nigeria, their giant neighbor. Until the 1970s, Nigeria's pre-occupation with internal matters and her peaceful foreign policy outlook have made her a force for regional stability. In addition, situated so far from the centers of power and conflict, and surrounded by relatively insignificant neighbors, "Nigeria is one of the fortunate countries that barely needs a foreign policy." [29]

During 1960–1961, two brief disputes were settled amicably, with Cameroon over the exact location of northern borders after British North Cameroon had chosen to enter Nigeria, and with Dahomey over the border sections dividing the Yoruba tribe. Both had the potential to become serious issues, and reflected perhaps as much about the inner problems facing Nigeria as about true foreign policy antagonisms: The Yoruba Action Group suggested the addition of Dahomey as a fourth region in Nigeria's federation, but Balewa's government disavowed any intention of pressing the issue.[30]

A visit by Gowon to Cameroon in April 1971 resulted in the settlement of the most recent border problems, caused by a series of incidents. Lasting peace in that area will depend heavily on Cameroon-Nigerian success in settling claims to off-shore oil, and on political stability in overcrowded southeast Nigeria, which Cameroon watches apprehensively.

Nigeria's more typical role has been as mediator, for example,

[29] Mackintosh, "Nigerian External Relations," p. 268. Samuel Chime, "The Organization of African Unity and African Boundaries," in Carl Gosta Widstrand, ed., *African Boundary Problems*, Uppsala: Scandinavian Institute of African Studies, 1969, pp. 74–77.

[30] I. W. Zartman, "The Politics of Boundaries," *Journal of Modern African Studies* 3, no. 2 (August, 1965), p. 170.

between Dahomey and Niger in their dispute over Lete Island in the Niger River. However, it should be kept in mind that postwar Nigeria, with its large, well-equipped, restless army, is not automatically the "force for peace" that it once was. A statement by an African student who commented during the civil war on the likelihood of Nigeria's neighbors recognizing Biafra is illuminating, though obviously based on a false prediction.

Many an African State, it is said, will not be entirely sad to see Nigeria made smaller, since its size has been a constant source of apprehension. There is no reason to place any credence on this view, especially as in the history of African affairs Nigeria has been as quiet as a lamb since 1960.[31]

It is likely that Nigeria's first regional priority for the 1970s, as part of a drive to reduce her dependence on foreign powers, will be to increase economic cooperation within West Africa. Again, however, it will be hard for Nigeria to forget the political realities of the immediate past. Fortunately for prospects of cooperation in the immediate areas of the Niger River valley and delta, the Francophone states of the area either refused to support French involvement in Biafra, or backed the Lagos regime outright. For Niger, a country which gambled by supporting Gowon's government in spite of her ties to France, the choice seems to have paid off. Soon after the war concluded, Nigeria rewarded the firm support given the Federal cause by Niger's President Hamani Diori by agreeing to a free trade zone with Niger. A landlocked country, Niger may now send exports through Nigeria to the sea, with possible reductions in cost over the longer trans-Dahomey route. It now appears that Nigeria is willing to support Niger's cooperation even at the cost of the competitive position of one of her own main agricultural crops, peanuts. Nigeria will receive larger amounts of meat and cement, while fuel oil will travel North.[32]

It is possible that Niger-Nigeria cooperation, which seems well-

[31] Chime, "The Organization of African Unity and African Boundaries" p. 77.
[32] Le Monde, August 5, 1970.

established on a basis of the 1970 trade agreement and earlier treaties on uses of Lake Chad and the Niger River, will make cooperation more difficult between Nigeria and Dahomey. Dahomey served as Niger's avenue to the sea during the colonial period and since independence, and will require some reconciling to the new arrangement. The May 1972 economic ties between Togo and Nigeria show the general concern for unity in the area.

Regional cooperation over the specific problems of infrastructural development and trade is certainly necessary if Nigeria wishes to lessen her dependence on the developed countries for trade. Less than 1 percent of Nigeria's trade has been with the 14-state West African region. There are some dangers in the reduction of economic barriers within the region: With 60 percent of West Africa's population, Nigeria could become the market for inexpensive manufactured goods from her neighbors. Thus, Nigeria will no doubt attempt to build her own light manufacturing, along with feasible heavy industry.[33]

One further question that deserves watching is Nigeria's attempt to improve the lot of the 100,000 Nigerians, mostly Ibo, who work on the Equatorial Guinean island of Fernando Po. A labor agreement signed in May 1971 attests to the improved dialogue between the two countries, soured during the civil war by Equatorial Guinea's role in providing relief flights to Biafra.

The prospects for Nigerian foreign policy are not easy to assess. From a position of physical weakness, questionable political non-alignment, and internal turmoil, Nigeria achieved a highly constructive image in foreign policy until diverted by the civil war. It is hard to tell what will be the impact on Africa's tropical giant of postwar suspicions of foreigners and desire for greater self-sufficiency. At the time of this writing, Nigeria's recent initiatives point to increased significance in African and world affairs, even while basic internal issues remain undecided.

---

[33] Adebayo Adedeji, "Prospects of Regional Economic Co-operation in West Africa," *Journal of Modern African Studies* 8, no. 2 (July, 1970).

Selected Bibliography

Geography, Traditional Systems, Early Contact with Europe

ANENE, JOSEPH C., *Southern Nigeria in Transition, 1885–1906*, New York: Cambridge University Press, 1965.

AYANDELE, E. A., *The Missionary Impact on Modern Nigeria, 1842–1914*, New York: Humanities Press, 1967.

BASCOM, WILLIAM, "Some Aspects of Yoruba Urbanization," *American Anthropologist*, 64, 1962.

BIOBAKU, SABURI O., *The Egba and Their Neighbors, 1842–1872*, Oxford: Clarendon Press, 1957.

BOHANNAN, PAUL, "A Man Apart, Tiv Tribesman," *Natural History*, 77, no. 8, 1968.

BRADBURY, R. E., *The Benin Kingdom and the Edo-Speaking Peoples of Southwestern Nigeria*, London: International Publications, 1964.

COHEN, RONALD, *The Kanuri of Bornu*, New York: Holt, Rinehart and Winston, 1964.

COHEN, RONALD, "Social Stratification in Bornu," in Arthur Tuden and Leonard Plotnicov, eds., *Social Stratification in Africa*, New York: Free Press, 1970.

DIKE, K. O., *Trade and Politics in the Niger Delta, 1830–1885*, London: Oxford University Press, 1956.

FLINT, JOHN, *Sir George Goldie and the Making of Nigeria*, London: Oxford University Press, 1960.

FORDE, DARYLL, and KABERRY, P. M., eds., *West African Kingdoms in the Nineteenth Century*, London: Oxford University Press, 1967.

GREEN, M. M., *Ibo Village Affairs*, New York: Praeger, 1964.

HILL, POLLY, *Rural Hausa*, London: Cambridge University Press, 1972.

HOGBEN, SIDNEY J., and KIRK-GREENE, A. H. M., *The Emirates of Northern Nigeria*, London: Oxford University Press, 1966.

JOHNSTON, H. A. S., The Fulani Empire of Sokoto, New York: Oxford University Press, 1967.

MINER, H., "Culture Change Under Pressure: A Hausa Case," Human Organization, 19, 1960.

NADEL, S. F., A Black Byzantium, London: Oxford University Press, 1942.

OTTENBERG, SIMON, "Ibo Receptivity to Change," in W. Bascom and M. J. Herskovits, eds., Continuity and Change in African Cultures, Chicago: University of Chicago Press, 1959.

SMITH, M. G., Government in Zazzau, London: Oxford University Press, 1960.

SMITH, MARY, Baba of Karo: A Woman of the Moslem Hausa, New York: Praeger, 1964.

UCHENDU, VICTOR C., The Igbo of Southeast Nigeria, New York: Holt, Rinehart and Winston, 1965.

UDO, REUBEN K., The Geographic Regions of Nigeria, London: Heinemann, 1970.

Historical Surveys, Colonial Period

AJAYI, J. F. A., Milestones in Nigerian History. Ibadan: Oxford University Press, 1962.

AJAYI, J. F. A., Christian Missions in Nigeria, Evanston, Ill.: Northwestern University Press, 1965.

ANENE, J. C., The International Boundaries of Nigeria, 1885–1960, London: Longmans, 1960.

ARIKPO, OKOI, The Development of Modern Nigeria, Baltimore: Penguin, 1967.

BURNS, SIR ALAN, History of Nigeria, London: Allen & Unwin, 1929.

COLEMAN, JAMES S., Nigeria: Background to Nationalism, Berkeley: University of California Press, 1960.

CROWDER, MICHAEL, "Colonial Rule in West Africa: Factor for Division or Unity," Civilizations, 14, 1964.

CROWDER, MICHAEL, "Indirect Rule—French and British Style," Africa, 34, 1964.

CROWDER, MICHAEL, The Story of Nigeria, London: Faber, 1967.

FLINT, JOHN E., Nigeria and Ghana, Englewood Cliffs, N. J.: Prentice-Hall, 1966.

KIRK-GREENE, A. H. M., Peoples of Nigeria: The Cultural Background to the Crisis," African Affairs, 66, 1967.

Nicolson, I. F., The Administration of Nigeria, 1900–1960, London: Oxford University Press, 1970.

OLUSANYA, G. O., "The Zikist Movement, 1946–1950," Journal of Modern African Studies, 4, 1966.

PERHAM, MARGERY, *Native Administration in Nigeria*, London: Oxford University Press, 1937.
PERHAM, MARGERY, *Lugard*, London: Collins, 1957.

Surveys of Nigerian Government and Politics: The First Republic

AWA, E. O., *Federal Government in Nigeria*, Los Angeles: University of California Press, 1964.
BRETTON, H. L., *Power and Stability in Nigeria*, New York: Praeger, 1962.
DUDLEY, B. J., "Traditionalism and Politics: A Case Study of Northern Nigeria," *Government and Opposition* 1967.
ENAHORO, CHIEF ANTHONY, *Fugitive Offender: The Story of a Political Prisoner*, London: Cassell, 1965.
EZERA, KALU, *Constitutional Developments in Nigeria*, London: Cambridge University Press, 1960.
EZERA, KALU, "The Failure of Nigerian Federalism and Proposed Constitutional Changes," *African Forum* II, 1, Summer, 1966.
FLOYD, BARRY, *Eastern Nigeria*, New York: Praeger, 1969.
HATCH, JOHN, *Nigeria: The Seeds of Disaster*, Chicago: Regnery, 1970.
MACKINTOSH, JOHN P., *Nigerian Government and Politics*, Evanston, Ill.: Northwestern University Press, 1966.
NIVEN, REX, *Nigeria*, London: Ernest Benn, 1967.
OHONBAMU, OBAROGIE, *The Psychology of the Nigerian Revolution*, New York: International Publications, 1970.
PROEHL, PAUL O., "Fundamental Rights Under the Nigerian Constitution, 1960–1965," University of California at Los Angeles African Studies Center, Paper #8.
ROTHCHILD, DONALD, "The Limits of Federalism: An Examination of Political Institutional Transfer in Africa," *Journal of Modern African Studies*, 4, 1966.
SCHWARZ, WALTER, *Nigeria*, London: Pall Mall, 1968.
SKLAR, RICHARD L., "Nigerian Politics: The Ordeal of Chief Awolowo, 1960–1965," in G. Carter, ed., *Politics in Africa*, New York: Harcourt Brace Jovanovich, 1966.
WHITAKER, C. S., Jr., *The Politics of Tradition, Continuity and Change in Northern Nigeria, 1946–1966*, Princeton, N. J.: Princeton University Press, 1970.

The Military Period, Current Governmental Organization

ABOYADE, OJETUNJI, "Relations Between Central and Local Institutions in the Development Process," in A. Rivkin, ed., *Nations by Design*, New York: Doubleday, 1968.

ADEDEJI, ADEBAYO, *Nigerian Administration and its Political Setting*, London: Hutchinson, 1968.

ADEWUMI, JAMES, *District Councils and District Council Budgeting in Ilorin Emirate*, Zaria, Nigeria: Institute of Administration, 1965.

CAMPBELL, M. J., *Attitudes Toward Development by Local Government in Nigeria*, Zaria, Nigeria: Institute of Administration, 1964.

DE ST JORRE, JOHN, *The Nigerian Civil War*, London: Hodder and Stoughton, 1971.

FEIT, EDWARD, "Military Coups and Political Development: Some Lessons from Ghana and Nigeria," *World Politics* 20, 1968.

GUTTERIDGE, WILLIAM, "Military Elites in Ghana and Nigeria," *African Forum* 2, 1966.

INSTITUTE OF ADMINISTRATION, University of Ife. *The Future of Local Government in Nigeria*, Ile-Ife, Nigeria: University of Ife Press, 1969.

KINGSLEY, J. DONALD, "Bureaucracy and Political Development, With Particular Reference to Nigeria," in J. La Palombara, *Bureaucracy and Political Development*, Princeton, N.J.: Princeton University Press, 1963.

KIRK-GREENE, ANTHONY, "The Merit Principle in an African Bureaucracy: Northern Nigeria," in A. Rivkin, *Nations by Design*, New York: Doubleday, 1968.

KIRK-GREENE, ANTHONY, *Crisis and Conflict in Nigeria: A Documentary Sourcebook 1966–1970*, London: Oxford University Press, 1971.

LUCKHAM, ROBIN, *The Nigerian Military*, London: Cambridge University Press, 1971.

MURRAY, DAVID JOHN, *The Work of Administration in Nigeria*, London: Hutchinson, 1969.

NIVEN, SIR REX, *The War for Nigerian Unity*, London: Evans, 1970.

OJUKWU, C. ODUMEGWU, *Biafra*, New York: Harper & Row, vol. 1, 1966; vol. 2, 1969.

OYINBO, JOHN, *Nigeria: Crisis and Beyond*, London: Charles Knight, 1971.

PANTER-BRICK, S. K., *Nigerian Politics and Military Rule*, New York: Oxford University Press, 1970.

TAMUNO, T. N., *The Police in Modern Nigeria*, Ibadan: Oxford University Press, 1971.

WILLIAMS, B. A., and WALSH, A. H., *Urban Government for Metropolitan Lagos*, New York: Praeger, 1967.

Social Structures, Political Attitudes, Communications

ABERNETHY, DAVID B. "Nigeria," in J. Scanlon, ed., *Church, State and Education in Africa*, New York: Teachers College Press, Columbia University, 1966.

ADELABU, ADEDEJI, "Studies in Trends in Nigeria's Educational Development: An Essay on Sources and Resources," *African Studies Review* XIV, 1971.

ELIAS, T. O., ed., *Nigerian Press Law*, London: Evans, 1969.

FREE, LLOYD A., *The Attitudes, Hopes and Fears of Nigerians*, Princeton, N. J.: Institute of International Social Research, 1964.

LEWIS, L. J., *Society, Schools and Progress in Nigeria*, Elmsford, N. Y.: Pergamon, 1967.

MARRIS, PETER, *Family and Social Change in an African City: A Study of Rehousing in Lagos*, Evanston, Ill.: Northwestern University Press, 1962.

OGUNSHEYE, AYO, "Nigeria," in James Coleman, ed., *Education and Political Development*, Princeton, N.J.: Princeton University Press, 1965.

OKAFOR-OMALI, DILIM, *A Nigerian Villager in Two Worlds*, London: Faber, 1965.

OKIN, T. A., *The Urbanized Nigerian*, New York: Exposition Press, 1968.

PLOTNICOV, LEONARD, "The Modern African Elite of Jos, Nigeria," in A. Tuden and L. Plotnicov, eds., *Social Stratification in Africa*, New York: Free Press, 1970.

VAN DE WALLE, ETIENNE, "Who's Who and Where in Nigeria," *Africa Report*, 1970.

YESUFU, SEGUN BABATUNDE, "Turmoil in an African University; Nigeria's University of Lagos," *America*, 1966.

Interest Groups

ALOBA, ABIODUN, "Tribal Unions in Party Politics," *West Africa*, 1954.

ANANABA, WOGU, *The Trade Union Movement in Nigeria*, New York: Africana, 1969.

ARDENER, SHIRLEY G., "The Social and Economic Significance of the Contribution Club Among a Section of the Southern Ibo," Ibadan, Annual Conference, West African Institute of Social and Economic Research, 1953.

BASCOM, WILLIAM, "The Esusu: A Credit Institution of the Yoruba," *Journal of the Royal Anthropological Institute*, 1952.

BRETTON, HENRY L., "Political Influence in Southern Nigeria," in H. J. Spiro, *Africa: The Primacy of Politics*, New York: Random House, 1966.

COLEMAN, JAMES S., "The Role of Tribal Associations in Nigeria," Ibadan, Annual Conference, West African Institute of Social and Economic Research, 1952.

COMHAIRE-SYLVAIN, SUZANNE, "Associations on the Basis of Origin in Lagos—1951," *Le Travail des Femmes à Lagos*, Zaïre, 1950.

LEITH-ROSS, SYLVIA, "The Rise of a New Elite Amongst the Women of Nigeria," *International Social Science Bulletin*, 1956.

LEITH-ROSS, SYLVIA, *African Women*, New York: Praeger, 1965.

MINERS, J. J., *The Nigerian Army, 1956–1966*, London: Methuen, 1971.

OFFODILE, E. P. OYEAKA, "Growth and Influence of Tribal Unions," *West African Review*, 1947.

OLUSANYA, G. O., "Ex-Servicemen in Nigerian Politics," *Journal of Modern African Studies*, 1968.

OTTENBERG, PHOEBE V., "The Changing Economic Position of Women Among the Afikpo Ibo," in W. Bascom and M. J. Herskovits, eds., *Continuity and Change in African Cultures*, Chicago: University of Chicago Press, 1959.

OTTENBERG, S., "Improvement Associations Among the Afikpo Ibo," *Africa*, 1955.

SMOCK, AUDREY, *Ibo Politics—The Role of Ethnic Unions in Eastern Nigeria*, Cambridge,Mass.: Harvard University Press, 1971.

SMOCK, DAVID R., *Conflict and Control in an African Trade Union: A Study of the Nigerian Coal Miners Union*, Stanford, Calif.: Hoover Institute, 1969.

Political Parties, Elections, Leadership

ALUKO, S., *1964 Federal Election Crisis: An Analysis*, Onitsha, Nigeria: Etudo, 1965.

AWOLOWO, OBAFEMI, *Awo: the Autobiography of Obafemi Awolowo*, London: Cambridge University Press, 1960.

AWOLOWO, OBAFEMI, *Path to Nigerian Freedom*, London: Oxford University Press, 1966.

AWOLOWO, OBAFEMI, *Thoughts on Nigerian Constitution*, London: Oxford University Press, 1966.

AWOLOWO, OBAFEMI, *The People's Republic*, Ibadan: Oxford University Press, 1968.

AWOLOWO, OBAFEMI, *The Strategy and Tactics of the People's Republic of Nigeria*, New York: Macmillan, 1970.

AZIKIWE, NNAMDI, *Zik, a Selection from the Speeches of Nnamdi Azikiwe*, London: Cambridge University Press, 1961.

BALEWA, SIR A. T., *Nigeria Speaks: Speeches Made Between 1957–1964*, Ijeka, Nigeria: Longmans, 1964.

BELLO, SIR AHMADU, *My Life*, London: Cambridge University Press, 1962.

DUDLEY, BILLY J., *Parties and Politics in Northern Nigeria*, London: Cass, 1968.

POST, K. W. J., *The Nigerian Federal Election of 1959*, London: Oxford University Press, 1963.

SKLAR, RICHARD, *Nigerian Political Parties*, Princeton, N. J.: Princeton University Press, 1963.

Domestic Development; Problems and Policies

ABOYADE, OJETUNJI, *Foundations of an African Economy*, New York: Praeger, 1966.

ADEDEJI, ADEBAYO, *Nigerian Federal Finance*, New York: Africana, 1969.

BALOGUN, LEKAN, *Nigeria: Social Justice or Doom*, Ibadan, Yemesi Publishers, 1970.

Consortium for the Study of Nigerian Rural Development, *Strategies and Recommendations for Nigerian Rural Development, 1969–1985*, East Lansing: Michigan State University Press, 1969.

EICHER, CARL K., and LIEDHOLM, CARL, eds., *Growth and Development of the Nigerian Economy*, East Lansing: Michigan State University Press, 1970.

Government of Nigeria, Ministry of Economic Development, *National Development Plan, 1970–1974*, Lagos: Nigerian National Press, 1970.

GREEN, REGINALD, H., "Four African Development Plans," *Journal of Modern African Studies*, 1965.

HELLEINER, GERALD K., *Peasant Agriculture, Government, and Economic Growth in Nigeria*, Homewood, Ill.: Irwin, 1966.

International Bank for Reconstruction and Development, *The Economic Development of Nigeria*, Baltimore: Johns Hopkins Press, 1955.

KILBY, PETER, *Industrialization in an Open Economy: Nigeria 1945–1966*, London: Cambridge University Press, 1969.

MABOGUNJE, AKIN L., *Urbanization in Nigeria*, New York: Africana 1968.

MARRIS, PETER, *Family and Social Change in an African City*, London: Routledge, 1961.

MARRIS, PETER, "Slum Clearance and Family Life in Lagos," *Human Organization*, 1960.

Nigerian Institute of Social and Economic Research, "Conference on National Reconstruction and Development in Nigeria," Ibadan: N. I. S. E. R., 1969.

OLUWASANMI, H. A., *Agriculture and Nigerian Development*, Ibadan: Oxford University Press, 1966.

ONYEMELUKWE, CLEMENT C., *Problems of Industrial Planning and Management in Nigeria*, New York: Columbia University Press, 1966. ·

PEARSON, SCOTT R., *Petroleum and the Nigerian Economy*, Stanford, Calif.: Stanford University Press, 1970.

SCHÄTZL, LUDWIG H., *Petroleum in Nigeria*, Ibadan: Oxford University Press, 1969.

SOKOLSKI, ALAN, *The Establishment of Manufacturing in Nigeria*, New York: Praeger, 1965.

STOLPER, WOLFGANG, *Planning Without Facts*, Cambridge: Harvard University Press, 1966.

YESUFU, T. M., ed., *Manpower Problems and Economic Development in Nigeria*, New York: Oxford University Press, 1971.

Foreign Affairs

ANGLIN, DOUGLAS, "Nigeria: Political Non-alignment and Economic Alignment," *Journal of Modern African Studies*, 1964.

IDANG, GORDON J., "The Politics of Nigerian Foreign Policy: The Ratification and Renunciation of the Anglo-Nigerian Defense Agreement," *African Studies Review*, 1970.

PHILLIPS, CLAUDE S., *The Development of Nigerian Foreign Policy*, Evanston, Ill.: Northwestern University Press, 1964.

Periodicals

Journal of Business and Social Studies (Lagos)
Nigerian Journal of Economic and Social Studies (Ibadan)
Nigerian Opinion (Ibadan)
West Africa (London)

Index

73 74 75 76   9 8 7 6 5 4 3 2 1

165